America's Unsung Heroine

WAITRESS

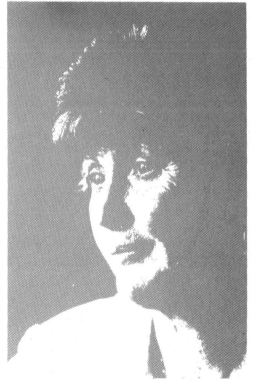

WAITRESS
America's Unsung Heroine

LEON ELDER & LIN ROLENS

CAPRA PRESS

1985

Cover design by Trish Reynales
Cover photo by Cara Moore
Book design by Francine Rudesill
Typography by Jim Cook

LIBRARY OF CONGRESS CATALOGUING IN PUBLICATION DATA
Young, Noel.
WAITRESS: AMERICA'S UNSUNG HEROINE.
1. Waitresses—United States—Interviews.
I. Rolens, Lin.   II. Title.
HD6073.H82U59   1985   331.7'616472   85-7874
ISBN 0-88496-235-0 (pbk.)

CAPRA PRESS
Post Office Box 2068, Santa Barbara, Ca. 93120

Table of Contents

Foreword

by Leon Elder

A waitress burst into tears when I sent back a cold bowl of soup. I was flabbergasted to see her break down. She was a veteran who daily heard other people's tales of woe, mothered their idiosyncracies and humored their spites and grievances. My first thought was tragedy in her home life—a stricken grandchild, husband lost his job. When she came back with the hot soup she told me sheepishly that one of her regulars, "Dear old Mister Hodges, keeled over in the street yesterday and was a goner even before the ambulance came. I just can't keep my mind on my work today, I'm going to miss that man. And you know what, he always liked his soup cool."

Having lived much of my life at the tender mercy of waitresses, having been pampered and abused, entertained and mystified, armed and oft smitten, I felt the time has come to hear it from them. They are the unsung heroines of our culture, responding to the hungers, thirsts, lusts and a thousand other more subtle needs with an equanimity that sometimes belies their own vulnerability.

That gave me some insight into what a true waitress is—a woman with a strong mothering sense who gets genuine satisfaction sending you back out the door better off than when you arrived. She cares. Many waitresses, out of modesty, would protest my observation and claim they were in it for the money, or the bunions. But I hold to my contention in spite of their blushes.

What intrigued me from the beginning was the waitress mystique. They come in all sizes and shapes, from schoolgirls to grandmothers. You can hardly go anywhere without encountering them, day or night, on the road or back home. There must be ten million of them in establishments all over America, from glitzy restaurants to dusty truck stops, from revolving coronas atop skyscrapers to fern havens under the streets, in pancake houses, cafeterias, diners, airport franchises, convention halls, and drugstores, as well as all the taverns, watering holes and jazz clubs where people go to be fed and quenched. When Manhattan goes to lunch 15,000 waitresses jump into action.

I was told that one out of five women have, at one time or another, been a waitress. While that may be factually true, only one in a hundred of those had the temperament or ability to stick it out and make it a career. Waitressing as a calling requires certain talents, both of heart and limb. Pedometer readings show the average waitress logs eight to ten miles a shift. Besides strength and stamina, she needs coordination and the willingness to endure hot plates on outstretched arms and the wit to parry the wise guy while struggling with a tray loaded with blue plate specials. Not every woman was conceived to endure so much physical and mental stress and to emerge with flying colors.

I have tried to imagine doing the job myself, but know I could never finish a shift. I'd be buffaloed by the side work before I even waited on real people. Mastering the lotus napkin fold would be beyond me. I wouldn't have the patience to top off the mustards, catsups, salts and creamers. The set-ups would demand a sense of order and uniformity contrary to my nature. No, I'm too unruly to be a waitperson. What mystifies me most of all is how a waitress can run the gamut of gaping mouths, lascivious cooks, truculent bartenders, paranoid owners, indolent busboys and hot plates and still be Miss Cheerful. That's the eternal mystery.

I would also think that dealing with people eating all day would get tiresome, coping with dirty plates and spills and still being able to bounce forward with the afterdinner mints and a bright "Come again, sir."

I am beholden to the bright-eyed waitress when she sees you coming and keeps you in sight. The genuine waitress has the peripheral vision of a basketball player and the anticipation of a quarterback. Have you ever had the feeling that she had your number from the moment you walked in and that menus and discussion were superfluous? I can hear her mind, "Ah, here comes Mr. Belgian Waffle with a fruit cup and black decaf. Coming right up, sir." It becomes a question whether she's reading your mind or instilling *her* ideas on your mind. Either way, you're at her mercy.

The array of waitresses collected in this book is to be representative rather than definitive. Nothing I could say about waitresses would be entirely wrong because among their millions you can find examples of every kind on earth. I haven't even gone very far out of my way, although a fair amount of traveling has given me heartfelt talks with waitresses in San Francisco, Los Angeles, New York, Dallas, Atlanta, Washington D.C., Key West, Chicago and dozens of small towns. The journeying has been haphazard over the past five years and I'm pleased to report that every waitress has been unique. While that revelation comes as no surprise, I am fascinated by certain similarities. If I were addressing a roomful of waitresses and asked everyone to raise her hand who got started in waitress work during the summer of her fifteenth year, I would quickly behold a sea of hands. Yet each of these fifteen-year-olds had her own waitress destiny, moving out into the world of eating and drinking establishments, from the most grand to the most mean. Waitresses are often required to fulfill someone's fantasy and wear an unseemly costume, from starched institutional jumpers to net stockings and miniskirts. Of my favorites is a native California soccer player whose mother was descended from the Japanese and gave her the gift of Oriental features. She took a job at an exclusive *sushi* restaurant where she served people sitting on mats in *tatami* rooms. She was willing to play the role of a good geisha, but her knees were killing her. Obeisance was hard on the knees until she thought to wear her soccer knee pads under the kimono.

I once wandered into a restaurant where salads were served from tulip-shaped bowls and the waitresses were made to wear several layers of starched cloth, wooden clogs and peaked caps. They even had rouge rubbed into their cheeks so they resembled the strumpets depicted in early Flemish painting. Skirts and petticoats were full and flouncy but blouses revealed an exaggerated decolletage. The busgirl who served me icewater and a basket of buns had such a look of exasperation I was prompted to ask how she liked working there. "This is my last day," she snorted. "If you think I'd wear this absurd outfit another day you're crazy. They don't even wear this stuff in Holland."

Generally, though, if dress requirements are comfortable and not demeaning, most waitresses have no complaints. "We're supposed to *look* like waitresses, after all," one declared. "Just as long as it doesn't get too militaristic." "Militaristic" may characterize policies enforced by some restaurant chains. They treat the waitress recruit as though she couldn't walk and talk at the same time. For starters the recruit is issued an employee handbook that must be sworn to and signed for. In its 75 pages it lays down the laws governing dress and grooming, behavior, job description, portion control, china and glassware breakage along with countless enjoinders. The waitress is furnished a company apron with her name badge, but is expected to buy shirt, pants and bow tie in conformance with company policy. Hair must be neat and shampooed regularly, heavy makeup or perfume is disallowed, nail polish allowed only in natural shades. Waitresses are expected to bathe daily, brush their teeth and use deodorant. They are also reminded that chewing gum is "unsightly and unprofessional." The *Employee Handbook* is indeed a manifesto with hundreds of house rules to learn and agree to in writing. Every piece of china or glassware is priced with the warning that one tray load of dishes dropped on the floor could wipe out the day's profit. (Customers are called "guests," although they are quite ready to cheer and applaud the sound of crashing dishes. I've never exactly understood why.)

While waitressing for the chains may be against the temperament of some women, others find comfort in the security and benefits offered by these giants. To illustrate the "generosity" of one chain, examine the following Employee Meal Plan. "The employee is entitled to receive a meal from the employee menu for each meal period worked at a cost of twenty-five cents per hour worked. All employees are entitled to an authorized thirty minute break on company time. . ."

The happiest waitresses seem to be found in long established family restaurants where everyone, from owner to dishwasher, turns out for the Sunday softball game and where New Year's Eve tips go into a common bucket to serve a good cause such as a waitress's new baby or an Easter picnic. Any restaurant called *Joe's* that declares the year it was established, is bound to breed camaraderie and offer waitresses at their best.

In so many of my conversations with waitresses, I detected a note of defensiveness which I find disturbing. After all, they are better paid than most shopclerks, secretaries and many professionals; they have certain esteem from their customers and are usually well liked. What's the problem? A good waitress is a blessing. She has brightened my day thousands of times, brought me playfulness along with the food, given me an ear, counsel and often a good joke. Though she has everything to be proud of, she is sometimes defensive about her job.

I know a good bar piano player, a man, who thoroughly enjoys his lot but hides his calling from his aged mother who raised him to be an industrial chemist. "It would break her heart if she found out I was doing this," he told me. I've heard waitresses say almost the same thing. It's not how they feel about waitressing, but how other people, particularly their parents, perceive their work. In the mind of seasoned restauranteur, Craig Bigelow, when college girls came into waitressing in the late 60s, the working class stigma largely disappeared. Still. . .

I wanted to include stewardesses in this book. They are flying waitresses, after all, and have us even more in their mercy than ground waitresses do. But none of the stewardesses I approached could be persuaded to be included in a waitress book. "We're flight attendants, not waitresses," one declared testily, showing that the social stigma has not disappeared entirely. "We are *professional*. We have been trained—upsidedown and in pitch blackness under water—how to open the door of a 747 and evacuate passengers." Waitressing, per se, was beneath their dignity, although that's all I've ever seen them do. Fortunately, I've never been in a situation where their higher training was needed.

Meanwhile, back on earth, waitresses can conceal or reveal many hidden talents. I was particularly startled one day when Sue Ann, a cheery woman with a braid in her hair and bands on her teeth, came bouncing up with a brighter smile than usual. "Notice anything different?" she asked. Of course, her bands were gone. "After three years it's like being let out. I'm free! Now I'm off to Carnegie Hall." She burst into a brief but glorious aria to demonstrate once and for all she had the voice of an angel. All the time I'd known her, she had been a closet singer as far as I knew. She had never told me she was the star of her class at the local music academy.

True to her word she traveled to New York, sang in Carnegie Hall and landed a role with a professional opera company. Some years later, while on tour, she looked in on the cafe where I'd known her. For the cafe gang, it was like family reunion. "I'm still hopping tables," she told them, "particularly in the off season. I'll always have that to fall back on, thanks to you."

She was perfectly willing to go back and forth between opera and the lunch shift and so are many other waitresses I've known—the novelist, the acupuncturist, the aerobics instructor, the marine biologist, the mother-of-four, the realtor, the law student, the bank teller, the tree surgeon, to name a few. Waitressing, unlike most other work, can be part-time or seasonal, with flexible hours and take-home money at end of the day. For some it's the perfect way to supplement another income; for others it's a way of life.

I've been asked why I haven't included waiters. Frankly, they don't interest me. I see that as another book entirely and leave the writing to a woman who has the same curiosities and infatuations about waiters as I have about my unsung heroines. Waiters come across as functionaries, businessmen even—impersonal, detached and efficient and not to be bantered with. Yet in all fairness, my hat's off to those dedicated waiters who come from the European school—all finesse, surety and hauteur. If I want brotherly advice or odds on a game, I'll consult a male bartender. Otherwise, the waitresses, bless them all, have captured my heart. Even if they occasionally spill, or fluster and get things wrong, they seem to have more stories to tell. I'm a happy listener and enjoy the flirtations. Without waitresses (I'm unabashed), I'd be lost.

If I'm alone in a strange town where else can I find a friend and get my lamb chops at the same time? The only other place is the hospital. Saintly as nurses are, patients only long to be released.

In waitresses I've found all kinds of womanhood as they relate to me and my fantasies—mother, sister, daughter, lover, *bruja* and concubine. Moreover, there have been friends and confidantes. We have shared secrets just as strangers can become intimates on a bus ride and never see each other again. I've learned a lot about passions and fantasies.

Some of the confidences are simply sad. A veteran waitress I shall call Beth had been married to a truck driver for thirty years and reached the point where her marriage was "worn out." At the same time a romance developed between her and the chef. They even planned to run off to Arizona and start life over. But as fate would have it, Beth's husband developed cancer and her romance with the chef was overcome by a great feeling of caring that welled up in her. Not only did she lose the desire to leave her husband, she even fell in love with him all over again and took care of him as she had never before. That's how she explained it to me, that capacity for caring that makes a true waitress.

Some men, certainly not all, share my affection and fascination for waitresses. When they come alone into a saloon or lunch counter, they don't sit at a table or at the middle of the bar. They find the end stool next to the waitress's station where she turns in orders and pops the fixings into highballs. They're back and forth every few minutes, and loiter there during slack moments. Here the devout waitress-lover has his conversational opportunities. Over an hour or so those fifteen-second chats often add up to a meaningful conversation.

I have unbounded admiration for a fifty-eight-year-old grandmother who works at my favorite watering hole. She tells me her life in bits and pieces as I sit on the end stool. She got her first waitress job when she was fifteen, and now, forty-three years and three husbands, four children and six grandchildren later, she's still at it. As she said, "My new husband has good investments and there's no need to keep working. But what would I do at home? This is my life, my big, big family." And after a day of serving people downtown, she goes home and makes supper for her husband.

Little more needs to be said. It's time the waitresses do the talking. This is a compilation of their testimony. Although many have common experience and tended to echo what another had said, I found that with careful listening or lucky prompting, each had something special to say. My gratitude is to them forever. Several professional photographers joined me on certain excursions or made forays of their own. Otherwise, with my apologies, the photography is my own with one of those fully automatic miniatures that lets you shoot from the hip.

If any one waitress inspired me to get this book under way, it was that teacher and book critic, Lin Rolens, who toiled as a waitress for ten years before my very eyes and led me to understand what a profound influence waitresses can have on us all.

Now it's time for her, and the others, to speak...

How the Harvey Girls Won the West

The art of waitressing was brought West by the Harvey Girls in the 1880s. Recruited by ads in Eastern papers inviting "attractive and intelligent young women of good character," they came West to be trained by restaurateur Fred Harvey at a starting salary of $17.50 a month. Harvey's waitresses presided at the Harvey Houses along the Atchison Topeka & Santa Fe Railroad. In starched uniforms, ironed to a fare-thee-well, "decorous and demure but drilled like soldiers in the proper way to serve a meal," these Harvey Girls, during their heyday, served 15 million meals a year.

"To this day, I can't stand to see a knife blade pointing outward," said Vernon Downes, 76, who was a Harvey Girl in 1926. "It's a very tiny thing, but when they throw the silver down in front of you, I just can't stand that. A lot of things I notice now, even in a real nice place—like where the glass of water goes, the bread and butter dish, the silver. They just put them any place. They don't know where they go. Old as I am, I still remember."

Harvey Girls were trained to serve a trainload of passengers five-course meals in twenty-five minutes. They weren't "hash-slingers" at all. They were deft as a surgeon with a scalpel as they boned a fish at table or carved a grapefruit so that no diner ever bit into a piece of bitter membrane. They were trained never to violate the precept that the customer is always right—unless he refused to wear a jacket. The girls were under strict orders not to seat any coatless male who refused to don one of the alpaca jackets kept near the door for such occasions.

Although today Harvey Houses are all but gone (a few remain in the Grand Canyon and Death Valley National Monument), the civilizing of the West was accomplished as much by the Harvey Girls as anyone else. They actually stood inspection before going on the floor: shoes had to be shined, uniform neat and clean, and they could not wear much makeup. Most of all, hands were inspected since they were noticed by the guests when food was served.

"You know, people kind of looked down on a girl for being a waitress in those days," recalled Opal Sells Hill, 84, a Harvey Girl for more than 45 years. "But they sure didn't when you worked for Fred Harvey!"

During her long career, Hill served many celebrities, including John D. Rockefeller, who tipped her a dime, and Will Rogers, who "told me a little story that goes like this:

"In the early days, the traveler fed on the buffalo. For this the buffalo got his picture on one side of the nickel. Well, Fred Harvey took up where the buffalo left off. He should have his picture on one side of the dime with one of his waitresses on the other. They have kept the West supplied with food and wives for the last century."   —L.E.

What Every Waitress Knows

AN INSIDER'S VIEW

by Lin Rolens

Eating is the most intimate act we are encouraged to perform in public and it is, for most people, a time of remarkable vulnerability. Both Miss Manners and Amy Vanderbilt spend a great deal of space working out the formal rituals of eating. These rituals carefully codify the process, make it safe.

When the public eats out, the person serving acts as guide. The waiter uses his masculine authority to maintain a distance, but the American waitress is a very different kind of figure. Always more intimate, she not only conducts you through the rituals of eating, but she serves, depending upon the need, as a Geisha-Nurse-Mother figure.

A roomful of people eating is a charged human atmosphere and a waitress moves through it as both participant and witness. Though it may be difficult to remember when you see her trudging down the aisle with plates stacked from her fingertips to her shoulder, this element of living theater is usually part of why she chose the job.

Over my ten years as a waitress, I watched people suffer major traumas and make important choices. As I ministered to them couples have sealed their engagement or decided to divorce. I saw people off on honeymoons and transoceanic holidays. I watched men kiss their loving wives goodbye and sip tall drinks while they waited for their mistresses to arrive on the next plane. As I poured the wine, gay lovers confessed infidelities, as did husbands and wives. I helped dozens of singles trying to have pleasant meals under the suspicious eyes of couples and families. The most powerful impression that remains is of the woman who ordered a grilled cheese sandwich and black coffee (always a bad sign) and sat twisting a well-used handkerchief as she waited for the next plane. She excused herself and rushed downstairs, apparently to the telephones. When she returned, I approached with her sandwich and poured a fresh cup of coffee. She looked down at the sandwich and then up at me and said quietly, "My mother is dead."

These may be extremes, but the waitress must be prepared not only to serve cheeseburgers and roast duckling, but to meet the needs of everyone who comes under her care. Sometimes people need only to be fed in a hurry, but more often she is needed for an intangible something extra. How many of us go out just for the ease of not cooking at home? More often, eating out is a special treat, a way of compensating for a lousy day, an attempt to stave off loneliness, or a time of intimacy with someone important in our lives.

A great deal of mothering goes on in America's restaurants. Any waitress takes particularly good care of her "regulars," those people who come in to eat with her on a fairly regular basis. She insists that they eat wheat rather than white; she may cluck a little when they opt for fries over a salad, and she listens to whatever they want to tell her.

Like the hairdresser, the waitress tends to personal needs without ever presenting that threat of serious interference. People spill their secrets and fears to her and they trust her discretion. In one little place I worked, a woman came in from exactly 4:00 to exactly 4:25 each afternoon. She was met by her lover and they would order white wine (which they never drank) and clutch at each other's hands and whisper tenderly. About every two weeks, the same woman would come in for Friday supper with her husband. She would always sit at one of my tables and smile calmly at me and then at her husband.

We asked one of the career waitresses in this book if she knew any secrets, if her customers confided in her. She smiled sweetly and assured us that a good waitress never sees or hears a single thing.

The nurse role in waitressing is closely akin to the mothering role; the primary difference is the customer's degree of need. People use restaurants as healing places to balm the wounds of the day or of their lives. Sometimes, they come in too wounded to know what they want and it is the waitress who suggests, who guides them into the oral solace they have been seeking. If they are not simply bent on drinking or eating themselves into temporary oblivion and if they are able to let her care for them, it is the waitress who will bring them around, who will assuage whatever pains they suffer. These "critical care" customers present the biggest challenge and they are rarely able to voice their thank yous. Such customers serve, in a sense, as the true measure of a waitress's substance; here virtue is its own reward for the only thanks she receives is the knowledge that she has, for the moment, made a difference.

The most socially suspect part of waitressing is the geisha role. Though it is equally accessible to women, most women have a difficult time receiving it. Most men delight in it: someone takes care of them and they can make small demands without having to take out the garbage or listen to what the children did today. And they can play. A waitress is one of the few people in this world with whom you can play without being trusted friends or without making extended courtly overtures. Much of the play that goes on is that harmless sexual banter that makes a feminist's skin crawl. Though most would not admit it, men like it because they can flirt and play without having to follow through. The great majority are grateful for this and I have lasting friendships that started with ritual flirtation over sandwiches.

A few men do mistake play for license and, if push comes to shove, a waitress can always refuse to serve them. But the waitress-as-wench error can usually be straightened out quickly, for their bravado is often thin. Such trespassers can usually be brought into line with a few serious words, a threat to call the manager, an offer to let them wear their order. On rare occasions, I delivered liquids into the lap of someone who just could not manage to contain himself. The response was always the same. The realization quickly comes that he had a beer-soaked crotch and, were he to make a scene, he, not I, would be the spectacle.

There is something very satisfying in the directness of tipping; if you please someone, do a good job, the reward is immediate. Most people manage to express their appreciation and the proof always remains on the table. They understand that you work for minimum wage (or less) and tip according to the current convention or according to how well you meet their needs. People tip in every spirit imaginable: they can be precise or reckless, begrudging or joyous; they tip to show off and they tip to preserve their discretion—and yours. They tip to demonstrate their power or to honor you and a job gracefully done.

And somehow, if you are not absolutely sapped for money, tips never feel like real money. Real money is ten or twenty or hundred dollar bills, money that can be used for something important like food or rent or children's shoes. But all those single dollar bills and fistfuls of change that weight down your purse hardly feel like real money. I have never had more pocket money than when I was a waitress. Somehow tip money manages to disappear and, amazingly, your purse is heavy again the next day.

Though the psychological aspects of waitressing may be the most interesting, the physical aspects are the most immediately real: waitressing is hard work. As a waitress you learn a great deal about your body. You learn to use the many surfaces of your hands to carry things. You learn balance and carriage and what they do for eight hours on your feet. You learn a walk that gets you places quickly without looking like you are running. You learn about the veins in your legs; often aging waitresses bind their offending calves like ailing athletes. And you manage, if you can stay away from the food, to stay fit; after years of exercising my pectorals carrying full coffee pots, pitchers of beer, and armfuls of plates I stopped waitressing and over the next several months I watched my breasts slide relentlessly down my chest.

One part of her body a waitress quickly learns to respect and value above all others: a waitress's feet are like a pianists's hands. A woman may know her clientele and work better than any, but if her feet give her problems, she might as well go home. Those mini hot-tubs-for-the-feet must have been invented for waitresses; I hesitate to think about how many evenings I have pulled a chair up to the bath tub and sat with my feet dangling in soothing warm water.

Take a good look at the shoes of the women who serve you. Though she may show flair in the rest of her appearance, a serious waitress knows she cannot afford to be vain about her feet. You will find your waitress wearing nurse's shoes or substantial walking shoes, usually rubber soled, often laced up. Some women develop a system of inserted pads and supports. The unswerving goal is to support the foot, to coddle it wherever possible.

A waitress spends much of her day walking quickly in short spurts, carrying heavy and volatile loads. The job is to get places in a hurry without looking like you are in a rush. You must deliver full bowls of steaming soup, trays jammed with drinks and oversauced dinners to customers without spilling a drop—and you must do it quickly. This requires developing a walk that is all business from the waist down, but looks fairly relaxed from the waist up. A waitress learns to have her legs pull her along rather than falling from foot to foot. The shoulders stay steady and the suspension system in the legs and hips absorbs any up-and-down motion. Starting and stopping are part of the process; just when you get up a full head of steam, you must come to a graceful halt in front of the appropriate table. All this fast walking and stopping and starting wreck havoc on the legs and back; for most waitresses, something usually hurts.

The popular wisdom believes that the luxury of jobs like waitressing is that you leave your worries at work. Though you may come home with a few aches and pains, the pressures of the job itself stays behind. For years I had recurring nightmares about waitressing, but I was too timid to ask if anyone else suffered from such visions. When I finally worked up the courage to ask, I found that not only nightmares, but my nightmares, were common.

The easy dreams came after a single, particularly busy day. At night, in my dreams, I would work and re-serve each drink and entree and dessert until I worked from the first through the last customers of my shift. This dream never terrified me, but I always woke up feeling as though I had worked another full shift.

The real nightmare came after at least a day of frantic activity. It always started pleasantly enough: I worked at a tiny but lovely little restaurant with two tables. The food was excellent, the atmosphere intimate and relaxed. I served those two tables with grace and pleasure and the feeling was so congenial that I felt as though I might be having a small dinner for friends. As soon as I placed the last of the main courses before the diners, two more tables would appear. This was no problem; four tables is pleasant work for any waitress. Just as I successfully met the needs of the new tables, four tables would suddenly appear. This proved something of a challenge, eight tables, but I always managed it, and, just as the last main course went on the last table, eight new tables would appear and I would go scurrying. If I managed to deal with these new tables, more and more tables started popping up all over the place as walls of the restaurant pulled back. I would run frantically until I woke up shaking.

The real nightmares, of course, are the daytime disasters that have the quality of bad dreams. These are most common when you first start a new job and most happen on lunch shifts where a wave of anxious eaters hits like a tornado and an hour and a half later, they disappear as quickly as they arrived.

Imagine that you have eight tables for four, 32 hungry people in all. A typical single order of the 32 might be a rare roast beef sandwich on sourdough, toasted, with the mayonaise on the side. And hold the lettuce, but slip in an extra tomato slice. They also need mustard, the grainy variety, and horseradish if you have it. They want french fries with their sandwich and need catsup to compliment those greasy hot potatoes. And to drink they would like coffee, decaffinated, with milk, not fake cream—and they will drink several cups with lunch. The days when you have 32 such orders are invariably the days when you think you left the iron on or you remember you sent your kids to school without lunch money or you just cannot manage to hit fourth gear from a standstill in the time required. These are also the days when people need several napkins and there are not enough to go around. So you must trek out to the storage area and root around for more napkins. And the dishwasher forgets to do the forks, which no one realizes until you serve four chef salads.

These are the days when you feel like a drowning man and the harder you flail, the worse it becomes. There is no solace in the knowledge that it will be over in an hour and a half because you are sure that this lunch shift is the Sisiphean rock you are being forced to push uphill through eternity. Anyone who needs anything more than a full belly on these days will almost certainly be left wanting.

And then there are days when the whole day feels like dancing, when you move through your shift gracefully and you delight everyone including yourself. These are the days when you put out your hand, without even looking, and the napkins are there, when all your favorite customers turn up and they appreciate you and you are mother-nurse-geisha in turn. On these every-so-often days, you go home with a heavy purse knowing that you have given people everything they wanted and more that they didn't know they wanted until you offered it. On such days you feel proud to be a waitress and you rejoice in the world and your place in it.

Cattle Call at Gallaghers

After the stoves and refrigerators are installed, the cadre of inspectors have stamped their approvals, the licenses issued, the stools bolted down, the sign painted, and menus printed, a new restaurant lacks but one thing to open—a staff. In addition to bartenders, cooks, dishwashers, busboys, and hostesses, it needs waiters and waitresses. If, like Gallagher's in Santa Barbara, the restaurant plans two shifts from 11:00 a.m. to 2:00 a.m. with a capacity seating of 120, it must quickly assemble a staff of nearly fifty. Filmmakers, when needing a gang of extras in a hurry, put on a "cattle call." New restaurants in southern California have adopted that term and everyone accepts it with good humor.

The cattle call at Gallagher's occurred less than a week before they opened their doors. One Saturday, more than a hundred applicants assembled in the saloon wearing name tags. Their resumes were stacked in front of the two owners, Chuck and Craig, who sat at a raised table by the front door. As her name was called, the hopeful waitress had to stroll

down an aisle in front of the others, climb two steps, and face her interrogators. Beyond her experience, the owners wanted to see if she was poised and self-assured and, if hired, she might stay on for a reasonable length of time. They didn't want fly-by-nights. They also wanted to know if she had studies or another job that might conflict with schedules.

Gallagher's cattle call took about six hours. Those selected were given a copy of the employee handbook and were asked to report back in two days for orientation and training. This group of photos shows the waitresses being interviewed at cattle call and during their first days on the job after being "Gallagherized." —L.E.

CHRIS CONNOLLY
(Commenting on Cattle Call)

"The waiting around was a drag, particularly when the owners lectured us on protocol and ethics. I couldn't keep my eyes open. I like being busy, as you can see. A busy bar is my idea of paradise."

Lori Johnston

"Last Saturday night, my waitress nightmare came true. Here it was, the busiest night of the week, all the tables full with fours and sixes and people waiting. A new girl and I had the whole dining room between us and suddenly, smack in the middle of everything, she walked out. I couldn't find her checks, didn't know what was ordered, tables needed clearing, people wanting drinks and food all at once. I could only do my best and tried to hide my tears. But only one table walked out. People saw what happened and stayed. Whew! They even tipped me more than usual, out of sympathy I guess. You know, when I first took the job I feared the worst, but people turn out to be far nicer than I expected. After Saturday, I guess I can survive anything."

Claudia Stratford

After being asked the score of a football game being played on the overhead TV:

"Don't ask me about football. I've got my head full with booze and dirty ashtrays."

Jana Swedo

"After eight years being a waitress I welcome the change to bartending. It pays better and time goes faster. You have to learn to cope with the obnoxious ones and the rotten jokes. A waitress can escape, but a bartender is trapped. And you have a row of people watching every move you make."

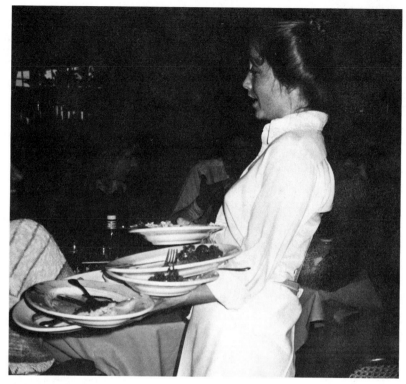

LISA HOWE

"When I was in high school I swore I'd never be a waitress—such a demeaning job. But I've found it gives me more money and freedom than anything else I know of. It also brings me camaraderie among the restaurant people themselves. I began as a hostess in a pie shop.

"I love to talk to people from out of town. Men are the easiest, but I have to be wary of the lonely ones who keep asking me out...

"I suggest everyone served leave a dollar tip and forget the 15 percent.

"Five years from now I'd like to be an entrepreneur and own my own corporation.

"I'm a germane waitress with a sense of territory.

"Older women can be a drag to wait on—they all want separate checks and leave grudging tips.

"I worked lunches for a restaurant that only hired men to wait dinners. That really pissed me off. At least test me for my proficiency."

NANCY HERSCHLER

"When you're a waitress you're an actress. You get into character and psych yourself up before you come to work. I got some of that as a high school cheerleader, I guess.

"Sometimes I get fed up with babysitting drunks. I served an underage oriental girl with an older man. They only had two bottles of wine, but she ended up in the hospital. Her life had been in my hands. When I heard, I turned white and started crying...I felt so responsible.

"You're a fool if you don't get along with the bartender. Don't bite the hand that feeds you.

"They don't want your boyfriends hanging around and you're not allowed to go out with customers.

"Be super nice to rude people—twice as nice. It might save the day.

"We trained to watch people for signs of overindulgence.

1. Make conversation and listen...
2. Do they try to light a cigarette from the wrong end?
3. Watch their eyes, bright or wavery?
4. Is their speech slurred?"

CATHLEEN ARIAN

"As a waitress, I would like to say I'm grateful to those customers who are friendly and who show appreciation. Since this is a public service job, the enjoyment and satisfaction from it relies partly on my customers. So, thanks to those who help make this job easier than what I know it can be."

"Oh Miss"

Karen Mead is unobtrusive and never seems either hurried or lagging. She's in perpetual motion, not unlike a veteran cowhand with her herd, getting her job done in an efficient and timely manner. She makes it look easy, slick as silk. If you want to be undisturbed, she seems to disappear, yet the refill comes just as you need it, or the check, if you're on the run. If you want repartee, she has a quick humor she can deliver without missing a beat, as evidenced by her name tag. Her regulars sing her praises. —L.E.

K AREN MEAD
(Popular family restaurant in a small city)

"When they asked if I had previous experience, I lied and told them I did, so they said, 'Those are your tables,' and shoved me out into the middle of the floor. Part of being a waitress is being capable of being brazen. Though I was only twenty, I had the energy and spunk to deal with the drunks and the late night rowdies. At 2 a.m. the place would be packed.

"It was a good place to start out because I was given so much latitude. It was a great place for me to learn how to react on the spur of the moment and not have to worry about it. It was also a good proving ground for my personality because I'd always held things in and never displayed anger. You can't do that as a waitress—you'd be crazed in no time.

"I've dressed down several people during my years here. Occasionally, someone would annoy me and I would lecture them, and most often it would increase the tip by a hundred percent.

"Looking back on those early days, I was pretty green. For one thing I wore an extremely short skirt that barely covered my fanny. At the same time I'd be highly annoyed if men made remarks about my legs. Here I was asking for all that masculine attention and then being offended by it. I wouldn't react that way today, but then I wouldn't be caught wearing a skirt like that either.

"Coffee shop training was great preparation for my job here. I learned how to work, and work fast. When I got here I had to learn about cocktails and a certain pretense of elegance.

"My personality has to change from table to table. Now I have a table of young men after work drinking, a table of old women having a nice quiet dinner, a family with little children screaming and carrying on, and then a table of nicely dressed well-to-do people who are trying to have a elegant evening. You have to balance all that stuff and be what they want you to be, a refined waitress, a saucy wench, and this and that. And you have to do it fast.

"When I go to work there's a subtle adjustment period when several shields drop down. Occasionally, someone will get to me before I get my routine in order and I don't react nearly as smoothly as I do once I'm in the swing of my work.

"He can be a dear, too. I was having trouble with a table one night, they were really being out of line and telling me I wasn't a very friendly waitress. They got to the point where they were perfectly willing to complain to the owner. Right on cue,

"I get along with the owner very well, but it's mostly because I stay out of his way when he's in a bad mood, and have a little fun with him when he's in a good mood. If he comes through the door on a rampage, he's capable of setting the whole place on its ear in five minutes time. He can disorient fourteen waitresses, twelve busboys, and two bartenders just that fast. Those are times I try to blend in with the wallpaper.

Harry came up behind me and said to them, 'What? What did you want to tell me?' They started complaining what a terrible waitress I was and he said, 'She's one of my best. If you don't like it, then get out.'

"Harry, the owner, deserves more attention. He's in his seventies and is really spectacular in his own despotic way. He keeps the chaos directed. He keeps everyone going in the same direction somehow. It's almost metaphysical. He's had this Midas touch since the beginning of his career, yet he really doesn't know anything about the restaurant business. He's never had to learn good business practices. He's always had customers to burn and plenty of people standing in line for jobs, so he's never had to be particularly careful how he treats either his customers or his help. One day he came in with the bright idea of attaching an adding-machine tape to every ticket. He'd seen this done somewhere. Fine, except there are only two adding machines in the building and both are a far distance from where you're working. So, if a customer stops you and wants his check, you have a long journey passing your other tables in two directions and hoping nobody will stop you for something. It was ludicrous, but we had to try it for a while.

"That incident when Harry backed me up, it was a party of five and this one fellow was particularly obnoxious. Harry's remarks shut him up. Most bullies are insecure, and as long as you're scared of them they'll keep on going. There's also the element of alcohol you can never, never forget because of the mammoth cocktails they serve here. People are different people at various stages of inebriation. They can be perfectly reasonable when they walk in the door, and be complete assholes by the time they leave.

"About waiting on women. Some are okay, of course, but when I see certain kinds come through the door I cringe. My least favorite thing about some women customers is those who whine. I just can't bear it. I'm prepared to give them whatever they want if only they let me know. A lot of

women, instead of telling me what they want, whine about what we don't have and you're supposed to deduce from that what you're supposed to do. It annoys me to the point of irrationality at times. The best way to circumnavigate this situation is to anticipate what they want before they can whine about it. So instead of having a squeaky-voice say, 'Can we have separate checks?' I'll address the table first and ask how many checks they'd like.

"The drawback to housewives is they tend to come in pairs and sit for a long time and not leave much in the way of tips. Sometimes there are those women that just don't seem able to read a menu. Either they never go out to eat or else they go out with their husbands who do the ordering for them. They want me to walk them through the menu and make the decisions for them. They'll ask, 'What's better, a top sirloin or a New York steak?' Which is strictly a matter of personal taste. One is more tender and the other has more flavor. I attempt to explain that to them. When I ask, 'How would you like your steak?' she says, 'Well, I'm not sure.' So I ask, 'What color would you like it when you cut it open?' 'Um,' she says, 'well, pink, but not red, and not too much...' It takes so much time and it's a delicate thing to try to coach them without getting impatient and to be the waitress they want you to be.

"I don't like waiting lunches. Very few come to enjoy a meal. They come either to do business or because they have to eat something so they're not starved by three o'clock. They come in, shove something into their face, and leave, little attention paid to the service or the food. Whereas at dinner it's an entirely different story with much more appreciation and leisure.

"There's a difference between new money and old money. Some feel that having money gives them the right to be obnoxious. But those with old money can be elegant and appreciative of a well-prepared and well-served dinner meal. I don't expect to be treated as an equal, but neither am I willing to be humble and servile.

"A waitress I know at a steak house in Los Angeles, a very reasonable woman, once had a party of nine—some kind of family gathering. A man among them was one of those who takes delight in making a waitress cry. Well, my friend would rather drop dead than cry. She put up with him through the whole five-course dinner and finally, when she delivered the check, she said, 'And one more thing. I hope that when you get up from this table that you take three steps and that your dick falls off and you step on it.' She was very lucky because

the rest of the party had gotten uncomfortable with him and they thought it was the funniest thing they ever heard. It released a lot of tension.

"People have certain places they want to

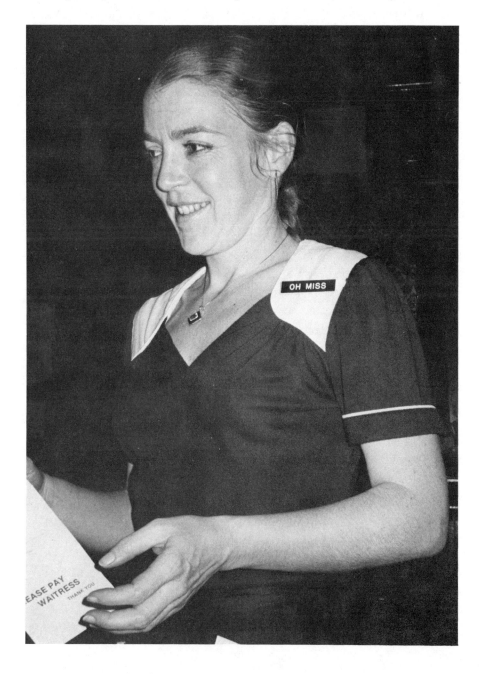

sit—I'm talking about regulars who want a certain booth or table—and if they can't have it right away they'll go stomping off. Our stock in trade is the regulars. We do get some tourists and casuals, but regulars keep this place going.

"Some waitresses have a cut-off point. They stop being good waitresses after a certain point. It's hard physical work but also hard mentally. To remain patient and tolerant in the face of all the things we've talked about. It gets harder and harder and harder. Some women stay waitresses too long and don't train themselves to do something else and they become trapped and unhappy. A poor waitress can ruin your meal. I've gone out to eat and been waited on by someone who made every least thing be such an effort. It was so discouraging. I'm not asking her to tap dance at the table, but just to be gracious and pleasant would be enough. They get too bossy and rigid and it somehow becomes the customer's fault that they're in this predicament. Yet others can do it all their lives and it stays fun for them. I'm not sure how much longer I'm good for—probably about five years.

"It's a good job for a single girl. Irregular hours, hard work.

"One night, a man celebrating his twenty-first birthday had gotten sick and vomited on the carpet on the way to the bathroom. The place was not lit and I was coming back from the kitchen with seven plates and I stepped in it and started to slide. My feet stopped at the edge of the carpet but my body kept going and, rather than crash into the table full of people, I elected to fall on the plates myself. It was a sorry sight.

"Being short, I sometimes have trouble serving plates across a wide table. It's a long reach and I have to balance the other plates. Sometimes people seem to be blind to the fact that an ashtray sits where you will set their plate. I hate to have to ask them to move their napkins out of the way, so I've taken to saying, 'Napkins in the laps, folks,' like my mother used to say.

"Another light-hearted thing I do is wear this name tag that says 'Oh Miss' and it's been a revelation. A lot of people don't get it and say, 'Is that really your name?' It gives my customers a way of calling me without tapping glasses or whistling, snapping fingers, or hissing."

Brief Encounters

These are the women we met once. Usually we were in transit or away from home on business or holidaying. In any case, these women were little oases of human contact as we bustled our ways through our own lives.

It is a measure of their trust that they spoke to us as candidly as they did. Most were glad to be asked about what they do and why they do it. Though there were common refrains, each had her own variations and her own insights.

—L.R.

BARBARA NASS
(Small city cafe)

"I began when I was fifteen and now, after thirty-seven years, I can't think of anything I'd rather do. This is my kind of place, a little touch of Oklahoma. We're all one big happy family, including the customers. My husband says I'm a better waitress than a cook. How's your coffee?"

Terri Blanchard
(Working alongside Barbara Nass)

"After working a full shift I like nothing better than sitting down and having the special. Yesterday it was meatloaf, but darned if we didn't run out just a half hour before quitting time. So I went home and made some—got my meatloaf after all."

L UCY JOSEFFINI
(Small garden restaurant near Hearst Castle)

"Waitressing is a centering for me. It satisfies my body, heart, and soul to touch strangers' lives, even if I never see them again.

"My father was a restauranteur in Northern California who never turned away a hungry person; that's become my credo too."

V ICKY RILEY
(A continental bakery serving breakfast and lunch)

"Although I come from New Zealand, the work isn't really that much different. Here the waitress is paid far better than she is back home and is treated a little less like a serving wench."

M ARY HINSLEY
(A chain coffee shop)

"I grew up in Iowa and started waitressing when I was fifteen. I do it because I like the people—you wouldn't last forty-eight hours if you didn't like people. Even the grumpy ones are okay because you soon learn that they usually have a pretty good reason for being grumpy.

"This weekend, on my day off, I'm cooking for a hundred at a church picnic— rolls and roast beef."

SUSAN MONTANYE
(A sumptuous bar with antique furniture)

"Last week we said goodbye to a waitress who'd been here for years. We took her into the alley out back and burned her skirt so she'd never have to wear it or wash it again. It was polyester and instead of burning it just melted away kind of sad. Waitresses can be so good to each other."

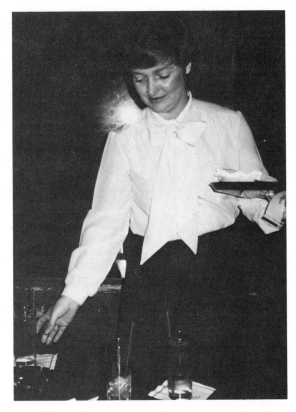

ARLENE FISHER
(Hotel cocktail lounge by the sea)

"I started at seventeen when my husband was an apprentice plumber and there wasn't much construction going on. I went to work to help out and then after the divorce I had to support my kids.

"My son pops off now and then and says he wished I'd done something more than be a waitress. But I tell him I've made a good living, it's an honorable profession and that pretty much shuts him up."

J UDY BROOKS
(Country French restaurant)

"My other job is landscaping because there are times I yearn to be out in the open by myself and not have to worry if my hands are clean."

MARY SONG
(A vintage country cafe)

"I got my first job as a car hop when I was fifteen: I lied and said I was eighteen. I'll never forget the first tray I delivered because I spilled a milkshake all over a man. He was real sweet about it.

"I've had other jobs like office work, but that was a drag. I always come back to this because I like the public and the goings on. I just like taking care of people; I have a husband and four kids still at home and I wait on them too—do all their laundry, everything.

"I've been here since 1972, over twelve years. We get mostly old timers here. In fact, they used to call this place the boardroom because all the farmers and politicians gathered here and talked over the business of the county. A lot of our customers are regulars. If they don't want their regular breakfast, they had better tell me when they come in the door because I'll have their order hanging by the time they sit down.

"I never tell anybody off. I come from the old school. One guy did proposition me once. I asked him why he thought he had the right to do that, he wouldn't proposition a nurse or supermarket checker. You have to be friendly to be a waitress and people will mistake that friendliness, but that doesn't happen too often. One guy threatened to punch me and I very cheerfully asked him if he'd like to drink his coffee or wear it—quieted him right down. But most people are just really nice to be around.

"My legs and feet hold up real well. The other day my feet hurt, but then I realized I'd written ninety-eight checks that day. We do a lot of side work here too; it takes an hour of our day. On Tuesdays we rotate the catsups and mustards and *Fantastic* the tables. Wednesdays we wash the windows, clean under the coffee machines and do all the booths. Thursdays we wash all the salt and pepper shakers and Fridays we wash the sugar holders. On Saturdays we just try to keep up with the customers. You may have noticed waitresses wash their own glasses here.

"We close two days a year—at noon on Thanksgiving and Christmas. We have a big buffet for all the families. We all pitch in and do it. We shut the curtains, lock the doors, and dance to the juke box. We have a grand time.

"I should tell you about some of the others. When I came to work here, Millie was our head waitress. She'd come to work right out of high school and wore this place like a glove. She must have worked here thirty-five years.

"Myra was here when I got here too. Her hair changed a lot. She was about my size, slow and easy-going, just the opposite of Ruby.

"Ruby was something else. She wore hot pants and had two-toned hair, red in front and white in back. She was from South Carolina and if she liked you, you got the best service in the world. But if she didn't like you, you could sit there for a long, long time. There she was in her sixties with hot pants and high heels, dancing with the customers in front of the juke box."

LILLIAN BLEUZE-NELSON
(Resort hotel with an ocean view)

"I've been a masseuse, taught yoga and done bookkeeping, but I make better money being a waitress. I like the physical work and thinking on my feet, dealing with people. I'm proud of the food here and I don't go home feeling greasy."

JEAN COFFIN
(The French Room of an elegant hotel)

"This is my first and only waitress job: I've been here for twenty-five years. My regulars come in year after year asking for my station; then they began bringing their children and now their grandchildren.

"Four gorgeous sisters come in regularly and make the whole dining room bloom. Everyone greets them, even the chef comes out. They're true, upper-class ladies.

"Who me? Retire? Never!"

JENNIFER KOUTLAS
(Neighborhood sports bar)

"I like men with a sense of humor. Amuse me and I'll amuse you. They tease and I tease right back. When some guy says, 'What time do you get off?' I tell him, 'About an hour after I quit work.' That naturally stops them. This work is good for the laughs."

MARILYN PIER
(Airport restaurant)

"Working in the airport I have great opportunities. Never know who you're going to meet. A great cross section of people, and if you need a good used car, a spare job or a place to live, you're going to run into someone who knows sooner or later. Everything that happens to me happens here.

"See those stewardesses over there? Bet they'd never be in a waitress book. They'll say they're not waitresses, but flight attendants, as though that was something very elevated."

[She was right. The stewardesses were testy and refused.]

BONNIE MENDELSON
(Las Vegas casino)

"Oh, they do rib me about my age. My pit bosses say I came over here in the first covered wagon and that they can see me in a wheelchair going around serving drinks.

"I've been working here for twenty-five years. I can hardly believe it, it's gone so fast. I even worked the first eighteen years without taking a vacation because I couldn't afford it, raising kids, having a housekeeper, the rent, the whole bit.

"It's hard work, running around and carrying these heavy trays all day long. I've always said you should pass an Army physical for this job."

L.A. TIMES

Los Angeles Times

C HERRIE THOMPSON
(A bowling alley coffeeshop)

"The only person I ever threw out was an obstetrician and his wife. He was rude and demanding as hell and had a reputation for being thrown out of every place in town. He wasn't a drunk either. An OB who doesn't like women—how do you like that?

"I quit school in the eighth grade and began as a waitress. I didn't want a sitting-down job. I always try to give the best service, even to the biggest bums in the world. Sometimes I even prefer the bums."

A NIS "SALLY" GERALDINE TERRY
(Dallas convention center)

"Conventions have their excitment—today the booksellers, tomorrow the plumbers, then the restauranteurs, hardware suppliers, and so on. I don't like the cosmetic conventions because they're mostly women. Men are a lot easier to wait on, particularly the hardware salesmen: they let their hair down and tell good dirty jokes."

P ATSY WELCH
(Truck stop featuring fresh cornbread muffins)

"Times were tough and the owner couldn't bear to waste food, even when it got stale. He recycled unsold muffins in the oven with a damp towel. One of my friends slipped a note into one saying, 'I was served this on Monday the 16th.' Four days later a truck driver bit into it—and got a free meal."

C AROL TIPPIT
(Dining room of a retirement home)

"After the turquoise and orange of Howard Johnson's, rotating customers every few minutes in the stark fluorescent light, my mind crammed with menu items and codes, this rest home became a sanctuary for me. Treading softly on beige carpet around six-seated tables of gray-haired ladies—I say ladies since they outrank the gents fifteen to one. Nice little old ladies, one dinner hour, one dinner, but no tips. These cute, little old ladies would have you believe they were as nice as they looked. But in fact there were some rather vicious seniors who split the dining room into definite factions. Most of the feuds were over the attentions of our one eligible bachelor, Mr. Ehlen. All of these women fluttered around him like bees to honey. I'd always know when he arrived by the mob of women clustering near the door, each reserving a seat for him at their tables. But he always shared it with a Mr. and Mrs. Knott.

"I collected much of the table gossip while serving the tables. I gathered the one woman most hated was Mrs. Quill, a woman who stayed mostly in her own apartment and often had dinner served there. She was beautiful, with soft silver hair, patrician manners, and very well traveled. The reason for all this peer hatred was because Mrs. Quill was Mr. Ehlen's choice. His eyes were solely for her. When she did appear in the dining room, they sat together—she in her elegance and he so debonair in his ascot, jacket and black-framed glasses.

"A story swirled through the dining room

one day. I picked it up from table to table. It seems that one of the ladies, when turning off her bedroom light, just happened to be looking across the ground at Mrs. Quill's apartment. There, framed in the window by soft yellow light, stood two silhouettes close together. One, of course, was Mrs. Quill, but the other, a man, was hard to identify. This woman continued her watch faithfully until the figures separated and came to the front door. It was midnight, quite late for this set. They remained in the doorway for some time, chatting intimately. Not until the man turned away did she recognize Mr. Ehlen. He hurried off before she had the sense to go out herself and question the man. This has been going on every night for a long time.

"Maybe not so much of a story after all, but it had the whole place buzzing for days. They need these events to keep them going, to keep their minds off the fact their homes are all sold, their children have their own families, and the fact that most of them are really alone and lonely. That's what makes this job so different from other waitress jobs.

"These dear old people also concern themselves with us, the young waitresses that come around every day. They have genuine interests in our lives, schools, boyfriends, everything. It's like I have about sixty grandmothers and a few grandfathers. Not so bad."

PATTI HENNING
(A homey bar/restaurant in the Sierra Nevada foothills)

"I love taking care of people as long as I don't have to take them home with me. I have customers who have followed me from the very first restaurant I've been in, which was nineteen years ago. Like today, a customer called, I didn't even recognize his name, and he says, 'We want your station, set it up for three because we love you.' When we have our own parties I invite a lot of our customers 'cause they're friends too. We all take care of each other. Tonight this waitress here made cookies. She didn't bake them just for her family, she brought them for her family down here. And that guy over there. He and his wife grow roses. They bring them to us free for the customers to enjoy with their lunch."

LILY
(Seaside hotel hostess)

"I've never met a stranger; I just join in with people. Even if the meal is bad, we're still able to make friends.

"I'd say that fifty percent of all waitresses are emotional and vulnerable—the rest just have their guard up. I'd rather wait on fifty men than one woman. Women seem to want something for nothing and they resent tipping you for what they do for free at home.

"I was born in Arkansas, quit school at fourteen, and went to New York where my sister was working as a waitress in Brooklyn. She got me a job there and I've been at it ever since."

TONI TARRACINO
(Key West saloon)

"Being the owner's daughter has its advantages, but not always, particularly when the college kids are here on spring break with their $20 traveller's checks, smashing beer cans against their heads and not leaving tips. Just between you and me, the military is no better.

"My dad gave me two rules: Don't take any hard times from anyone, and don't run tabs."

JEANIE
(Expense-account restaurant with Scottish motif)

"Although I don't have a drop of Scottish blood, I find myself almost talking with a brogue after all the years here. Being a waitress here is having a role to play. We have a busy, expense account, men's lunch; they are the best tippers in the world as long as you keep smiling."

RITA COATES
(A large hotel on a Pacific beach)

"I came over here from a Yorkshire mining town over twenty years ago. I spoke a broad Yorkshire that no one could understand. I filled in for a sick friend at a place called The Green Gables. In spite of my accent, they kept me on for years.

"Language still creates interesting problems; I had to invent a sign language for some Japanese men to ask if they wanted fish, beef, or chicken. I did this absurd pantomiming, flapping my arms and all, but they caught on.

"I love being a waitress in a hotel dining room where you get a sense of people's needs during their stay. Breakfast eaters are the pickiest. The poached egg is the killer; if there is one wrong wobble in that egg, you've got trouble. Americans love to dip toast in their egg yolks. And they are easy, Americans will eat things in any order;

however, Europeans want everything in a certain order.

"Now, if you've got four picky people at one table, and they all want their eggs different and different kinds of toast or muffins, buttered or dry, toasted light or dark, and then you try to serve them all together hot, it is only a bloody miracle if anyone gets satisfied. That's what I've been trying to achieve for twenty-five years.

"I always serve clockwise. But I'm totally lost if people change places after they've ordered. A party of eight switched completely one day; Dad wanted to be closer to the heater, Grandma wanted an outside seat, and the kids squirmed into different places. They created absolute chaos.

"Sometimes, when I get frustrated, I run into the kitchen and scream into the refrigerator at the top of my lungs. It feels really good, and then it's all over.

"But I remember one night when screaming would have made no difference. When I made a last call, this big party of people ordered fifteen of the most colorful drinks you could imagine—Grasshoppers, Pink Ladies, you name it. Fifteen of them. We had to wear little pink costumes, you know: backless, nearly frontless, and panty-hose with seams. Anyway, I was carrying this rainbow tray of drinks and this guy half crocked stopped me. I told him I'd given last call fifteen minutes before. He turned belligerent and tipped the tray over my front. I couldn't believe it: Irish coffee on my left side, Pink Lady down my chest, Grass-hopper down my right side, and beer, beer all down my legs. I didn't know whether to punch the guy or scream or cry.

"But most of the time, this is great work and I love it. I must admit that, after working for the public all week long, on my days off I keep the front shades drawn and work in the back garden. I need to be by myself sometimes."

Norma Lillard
(Low-lit restaurant near County Courthouse)

"I've been here twenty-two years and I have the best job in the county. Some women do it because of divorce—that's what they all say—but I've been married to a wonderful man I met here twenty years ago. He says I have to retire when he does, but I'm not sure I will.

"You learn to carry yourself like a waitress and people will respect you. They'd never say anything rude or aggressive. You get to take care of people all day: they might feel a little low when they come in, but by the time they go out, you have them turned around.

"I started in a diner in the midwest when I was fifteen. What gets me is I'm checking IDs on kids who were born after I came to work here. Seems like no time at all."

ANN BOARDMAN
(Working alongside Norma Lilliard)

"Waitressing used to be a shameful thing to do. People thought you almost had to be a prostitute. Some thought they could actually grab you and take you out and all, but over the years, and it's taken a while, waitressing has really become a profession.

"Years ago I was a resort waitress in Cape Cod and Florida. The chef would move his whole crew from one resort to another. We'd work all three meals seven days a week for twelve weeks straight then we'd have two months off. We really got along—like a family it was and we really knew each other. All you had to do was look at someone to know what they wanted. It was really fun. It gets into your blood, particularly after thirty-five years."

JENNIFER SMITH
(A novelty pizza house with antiques)

"The clown and I have our laughs. Most people I wait on seem to take everything so seriously. Really!"

RHETTA MASSEY
(A bakery coffeeshop)

"I serve croissants by day and work on symphony budgets by night. My dream, though, is to be an import/export wine broker."

MARY BURCH
(Arizona country saloon)

"It's a job. If you have to work, you have to work. I've been at it for fifteen years. I never drink when I'm working or before I come to work or after I get off. I have two days off a week; the first day I go out and drink.

"Today's crowd is typical for this bar; this is 'big ranch' country and is the main change-over for the Santa Fe Railroad. When there is a brawl, you do whatever you have to do—it's even interesting sometimes."

LORI OLSON
(A chic San Francisco rendezvous)

"If you want to raise the hair on the back of my neck, just let me hear someone say, 'This job didn't work out, but I can always be a waitress.' It's a profession, and you have to like it to be any good.

"What's it like being a waitress? Imagine throwing a dinner party but you don't know how many people are coming, what they're going to eat or drink, or when they're leaving or when other friends will arrive. You have infinite variables and somehow you have to pull it off. I try to look at it like I'm hosting a dinner party and we are all friends. Still, you can't be too familiar either.

"You must be an actress, improvising *every* inch of the way. You can come in feeling hung over, but you have to leave

those feelings behind. You try to appear effortless.

"It's part of my nature, being the last of six children, to be the observer of others. It's a talent a waitress must develop along with being a little psychic to see ahead and keep a couple of steps ahead of yourself. There's a certain kind of person who will sit down, and I know by the way they order and the way they look that, before I even get to the kitchen, they'll change their mind. So I won't even put the order in. I'll hang around a second, get them a drink, and let them reconsider. Play the people and the tips will follow.

"A lot of people don't have anyone else in the world to boss around. You can't harp on your wife, your boss, or your kids. But you can walk into a restaurant and have a maid for half an hour, and be picky about your food.

"When I go out on my free time and get waited on, it's like a doctor going to another doctor. I feel like I'm a terrible customer, and I can be very demanding because I know what a place is capable of."

TONI REECE
(An all-purpose restaurant in old downtown)

"These are English walking shoes. You can't fool your feet; these will last maybe two months, but they're worth it. On a hard day, we measured once, I'll walk about twenty-five miles.

"I like coming in at 5:30 in the morning and setting up the stations when I've got the place all to myself. It's my quiet time before the rush of the day. Then I turn into a tiger.

"Some gals work right on up through their sixties. We lost a gal just last week. Her husband was a bartender and they worked together for thirty years. She was 62, tall and beautiful, no one guessed how old she was. She loved it; carried plates on the day she died."

S HELLEY BATES
(Seafood restaurant on the beach)

"The trick here is to keep sand out of the food, but nobody cooperates. People track it in—it's in their clothes, their hair, even their eyebrows. And then they complain about gritty chowder."

E LLEN CHAN
(Airport restaurant)

"In Taiwan, a ten percent tip is included in the price of the meal. The waitresses there are not educated people and earn less than the poorest paid secretary.

"I'd rather work in an American restaurant. The Chinese restaurants here are mostly family-run, with long hours, low pay and no union.

"Airports are great place to learn languages."

SUZANNE SULLIVAN
(Greenwich Village hangout)

"In the summer we put tables on the sidewalk. It was a hot day, in the nineties, and everyone was irritable, even the dogs. A woman had tied her terrier to the parking meter and it was attacking every dog that came by. Two men were arguing and shoving each other around and suddenly a dog fight exploded under my feet. The lady who owned the terrier just looked the other way and paid no attention.

"The other woman pulled her dog loose and disappeared, but then she came back— you'll never believe this—with a bag of raw eggs. She marched right over to the dog lady's table and began smashing eggs on the table in front of her, ruining her meal. Splat, splat, splat! What a mess! Even the man at the next table got splattered, and he was in a neat navy suit. But he was nice about it.

"Anyway, it was a real mess, egg everywhere, dripping through cracks in the table even. The two ladies disappeared and guess who got to clean it all up? That's the joy of waitressing for you."

RYLEN LEE
(Premiere punk cafe that takes its anarchy seriously)

"It's wild how successful this place has become. You walk in here and it's not 'customer knows best,' it's 'staff knows best.' The whole atmosphere of this place—with art and things changing and the loudness—it's crazy, not somewhere to go for a quiet dinner. But it's really good energy, from the cooks on up. It's really

tight—it *has* to be, given how unorganized it is, and crowded. I'll be standing over there waiting for your drinks and I'll have someone's arm over me and under me and around me, and a bus-person barging through with a tray of glasses.

"Other places I've worked it's been really heavy having to *please* and kiss ass. But you don't have to here. Some people don't realize that if they're nice we'll give them so much better service; and when they're going

to be assholes, you just put their ticket last. Their food's not going to be as good and they don't get their drinks on time.

"It seems the ruder you are, the better they tip you. If you give good service and are rude in a sarcastic way, they find it humorous. It's all part of the atmosphere, because a lot of the people who come here are not young and trendy. Some are older people coming here for the excitement or just to *look* at us. The best tips I've ever gotten are in this place. I mean, we *average* twenty-five percent tips. It's because of the attitude. If you have to smile *every* day you get really boring.

"My boyfriend works here. He's the 'slam-busboy' around here, the total anarchist. Every week he has a different color hair. He runs around really mad and is always getting in trouble—going upstairs, getting stoned, and *almost* getting fired. He's a real character. Lots of characters here, like Jennifer too. She's your classic idea of a punk. She would show up with crucifixes and gigantic blonde hair shaved up on one side, the slowest bus-person you could ever imagine, but the customers loved her. She was window-dressing. I think a lot of people come here to have the punk scene de-mystified for them a little.

"Here we're seen as real people, not just freaky. I had an older, straight-laced *businessman* tell me my blue hair was *beautiful.* On the street they look at me with hostility. But here they're on my turf and it's fun for them. A lot of places people will treat a waitress like a servant, but not here.

"I once worked in a restaurant where I had to dress in uniforms, take off all my earrings, except one in each ear, keep my hair flat and wear my make-up mild. It just wasn't me. It diluted my personality. Here you wear whatever you want, usually the wilder the better. You get to dress up to go to work. On Halloween I dressed up in this wild Medusa costume. Even my friends didn't recognize me. And I can do that *any* night. I won't get any flack.

"It's spoiling me here, so much freer than anywhere else. Certainly I smile, I don't tell just *everybody* to 'fuck off.' But neither do I have fear of the customers as I once did."

—JEFF GREENWALD,
guest interviewer

Pauline Martinez
(Hollywood's classic Jewish delicatessen)

"I get a lot of older people, regulars, who come in and sit in my station. One fine gentleman says, 'You smile more at me over coffee than my wife does all day.'

"One old man came in for lunch yesterday, the usual thing: knockwurst sandwich, sauerkraut, and a Pepsi. He paid me at the counter then went over to the cash register to pay there too. Then he came in an hour later and wanted lunch all over again; I had to tell him he'd already had lunch. Another day he walked out without paying at all and I had to chase after him without embarrassing him. Everybody needs some kind of taking care of."

Suzanne Casanova
(A ferny chain restaurant)

"When I tried to card* a young woman—she didn't look a day over eighteen—the older man with her got arrogant and insistent. I asked the manager what to do, and he said serve both drinks to him. That is what I did."

*Check her ID.

JENI FRAAS
(Fast-food franchise on a wharf)

"We work in five-person shifts and customers make or break the day. Naturally, we get mostly tourists and a lot of them don't speak English, so they point a lot and we play sign language games.

    "There are six kids in my family and I'm number three and we've all worked here. I've been here for six years, so I'm the manager by seniority. I have to play the heavy, do the hiring and firing and all that. I'd never win a popularity contest."

DESTI CENTINEO
(Truck stop)

"I may look like a chicken with my head cut off, but I really know what I'm doing: I've got eleven tables working right now.

"I might have made better tips at Carrow's or Denny's, but I was just a dime a dozen there. It's different here because it's family owned. They know their business depends on you and you get the respect. We even got a Christmas bonus. That's never happened before. Imagine!

"I've heard every dirty joke in the world. The truckers treat me as one of their own; we're all working class together. You know the difference between a toilet seat and a waitress? A toilet seat only waits on one asshole at a time."

M ARY HAYES
(Small struggling cafe)

"This is absolutely historic, taking my picture on my first day *ever* as a waitress. Call this the 'before' shot."

J UDITH THRASH
(Airport cocktail lounge)

"We get the terrified fliers up here. They wait until the plane has been called and then they come up to the bar and order at least two drinks, usually straight shots. They pour these drinks down their throats looking hard at the airplane sitting in front of them the whole time. Then they slap a bill on the bartop and dash downstairs; the goal is to get on the plane before the drinks hit you, but to be anesthetized before the wheels leave the ground."

MARY ANNE DRISCOLL MURPHY
(New York haunt for writers and painters)

"My name gets more Irish as it gets along. We're supposed to be good storytellers, but I can't think of one. Just of the day when only two of us were waiting and suddenly all the tables filled up. We couldn't handle it, so we told people to go across the street— even the boss agreed."

KIMBERLY OBBEMA
(A popular art deco cafe)

"You have to put in a word of your own sometimes...."

NORA LEE YOUNGBLOOD
(Desert truck stop)

"Waitressing is about all I've ever done. I've known some of these drivers for years, but I don't even know one of them's name, not one. After you've worked so long, you see faces and that's all you see; I see so many in a day. This truck driver here, I've known him for twenty years: I don't even know his name."

DARLENE STADLER
(Dining room of a seaside hotel)

"I've had five kids and one husband, and I'm proud to say that I still have them all. My husband has been a deputy sheriff for twenty-eight years.

"My mother was in the business as a cocktail waitress and restaurant manager, so it seems natural to me. I started when I was fourteen; I lied and said I was fifteen. My first job was at an old-fashioned malt shop; we had twenty stools and it was all counter work—sandwiches, malts, and sundaes. I'll never forget the day I accidentally dropped a scoop of peppermint ice cream in the lap of an older gentleman. Without thinking, I reached down and plucked it up; everyone laughed except his wife.

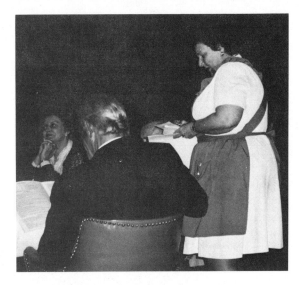

"We get tourists and salesmen away from home, and we give them someone to talk to without any threat. We take care of them, treat them like family, make them feel at home."

L IZ HAGAN
(Greenwich Village hangout)

"On my second day on the job, a woman and her boyfriend both asked me out at the same time. I thought they were kidding, then I realized they weren't. They were left-overs from the '60s and the communal existence, and they seemed genuinely *hurt* when I turned them down.

"People are always asking what I do on the side. I tell them I'm an actress playing a waitress on the side."

The Midge Poynter Story

Although comfortably married to a space engineer, Midge Poynter continues waitressing a few days a week and running a halfway house for stray and orphaned animals. She founded "Life-Line For Pets," a non-profit organization to shelter sick, wounded, and abandoned dogs, cats, and rabbits; Midge nourishes and nurses them and tries to find them homes. Yet there are always dozens of hungry creatures in her home and backyard. "It does my heart good," she says, in spite of veterinarian bills that average $300 a month. When she gets into arrears, she simply throws her annual potluck beer bust. During idle moments, she writes educational books. You won't find a nature more compassionate than Midge's—or more resourceful.

—L.E.

MIDGE POYNTER
(An unpretentious restaurant)

"I became a waitress the way so many women do: by default, out of sheer desperation. I was working my way toward a teaching credential, but it was 1945, a war had ended, and my Marine came marching home. True to the American dream of the post-war era, we promptly married and had four children in ten years. Before the last child was born, our dream turned to a nightmare: my husband left us for parts unknown.

"What does a college drop-out with no job skills do in such a situation? I started looking for work when my baby was six weeks old. A neighbor who was giving us 'leftover' food showed me an advertisement; a coffeeshop chain was seeking inexperienced women for a waitress-training program.

"I applied at one of their family-type restaurants and was stunned when they accepted me. There I was: twenty-eight years old, painfully shy, no work experience, no babysitter, and no transportation. All I had was a job working nights as a waitress.

"On a summer evening in 1955, I showed my hastily hired babysitter where the diapers were, checked my uniform one last time, and ran to the bus stop. Assigned to work the 6 p.m. to 2 a.m. shift, I had no idea how I would get home. All I could think of was getting to work, making some money for milk and bread, and hoping I wouldn't be fired before the shift was over. When the bus stopped in front of the restaurant, I walked back and forth for five minutes before I found the courage to enter.

"Nine hours later, I carried eighty cents in my pocket and had arranged for a ride home with one of the other waitresses. My uniform was splattered with chocolate from milk shakes and hot fudge sundaes. 'You're supposed to work *on* the fountain, not in it,' my boss said. He understood how frightened I had been when I first walked into his office.

"When I arrived home, I was at once achingly tired, but too excited to relax. Over a cup of tea, I thought about the experienced waitresses I had seen in action. I envied them their efficiency and the tips they made while I was drawing cokes and cleaning spills on the fountain. I could hardly wait to make eight or ten dollars a night: after paying the babysitter her five, I would have plenty for food money, and my pay checks would cover the rent and other bills.

"At the same time, I dreaded the time I would come out from behind the security of the fountain. How would I ever make it through a busy dinner? What if I mixed up the orders? And what if I should spill on someone? I pictured myself doing everything wrong. Would I be able to resist the temptation to walk out the back door and never come back?

"As I crawled into bed three hours before the baby was due to wake up, I knew that I had to resist that temptation. I needed that job: my kids were depending on me.

"I lived through that first week and the next and the next. For eleven years I worked the night shift, then transferred to the breakfast shift and also taught waitress-training classes. During that time, I did much more than support my four children in a reasonable style: I gained self-confidence and now I can meet anyone from any walk of life with ease. Among my customers were custodians and students from the city college across the street. I waited on professors from Cal Tech and brilliant graduate students from all parts of the world. I made friends with older retired couples and families with young children. And I met the man who was to become my second husband, who married me, not in spite of my children, but *because* of them.

"I learned about human behavior and how to handle difficult situations. The world doesn't stop spinning just because I spill a root-beer float on a little boy or dump a plate of chili beans in a man's lap. It didn't even stop when I felt my half-slip slither down my legs as I was carrying three hot-fudge sundaes.

"People are supportive and understanding if they see you are doing your best. The difficult ones stand out in my memory because they are so few. Some people come into a restaurant with a chip on their shoulder, but that chip disappears when they have had a few bites to eat. I call them my hypoglycemic customers—as their blood sugar rises, their ill humor disappears.

"Others, however, seem to have been born angry. They like to show their 'superiority' by making the waitresses' life as miserable as possible—and they leave the smallest tips. I survive their onslaughts by telling myself that it's better to *act* than to *react*. Why should I respond to their crankiness with more crankiness? I simply tell myself that I can be better than this ornery person. I can keep smiling while he's complaining about some insignificant detail. I can apologize for making a mistake in his

order when the mistake was his—how can I know he wanted cottage cheese instead of potatoes if he didn't tell me?

"I have a hunch that some of those people later realize their error and leave bigger tips to make up for their short tempers.

"I remember one customer because of his one understanding remark. It had been a busy Saturday night with an important high school football game. At 1:30 in the morning, we were getting the after-movie crowd and we hadn't even started our clean up. I gritted my teeth when a party of six sat on my station and ordered coffee, pie, and hot-fudge sundaes. Somehow I served them all, but my mind was on filling salt shakers and sugar bowls and getting home before the kids woke up. When I handed the bill to the man at the head of the table, he smiled and pressed a dollar bill into my hand. 'You did good,' he said. 'You're really tired, aren't you? Hang in there. It'll be over soon.' I doubt if he knows that a waitress still remembers him after all these years.

"It feels good to be part of a smoothly running restaurant operation. It is amazing how many customers we can serve and send on their way in thirty or forty minutes when other waitresses step in to help without being asked, when the food comes out of the kitchen in a steady flow, when the dish-room crew has the cups, saucers and silverware in the right place at the right time.

"On the other hand, I've seen plenty of slow afternoons and evenings, with a full crew, when nothing goes right. The cook bangs on his bell but I'm taking an order from a customer who cannot make up his mind. One of the waitresses drags her heels because she didn't get enough sleep the night before; the rest of us can't ignore her customers' pleas, but resent having to do double duty. On those days, the dishwashers seem to delight in piling up all the silver on one station and bringing out cups when we need saucers. My station fills up and empties all at one time, and one group of customers will be oblivious to the fact that I have four other tables waiting to be served. They either want to visit with me or they inquire about the latest baseball scores. (Why do people think waitresses know the baseball scores?)

"I like working under pressure, meeting deadlines, making every second count. To me, that's one of the big attractions of the restaurant business. And I like to feel really *needed*. When someone calls in sick, the manager can't say, as he could in an office, 'Oh, well, her work can wait until tomorrow.' The customer is here now and deserves immediate attention. If I don't appear to fill in the square on the schedule, someone else will have to. All good waitresses feel a tremendous sense of obligation to be on the floor when they're supposed to.

"I've found working helps me forget most of the common physical ailments; being around people and the hectic pace of the job don't leave much room for stomach cramps or a vague case of the 'blahs.' But, if I'm really sick, I know the manager will find a way to send me home as soon as possible.

"There are plenty of other reasons why I like being a waitress. Depending on my body clock, or the availability of a babysitter, I can work either days or nights. I like the feeling of being instantly rewarded when I do a good job; those tips indicate that I am doing something right. I like the people I meet and I like the physical exercise that comes with the job.

"Mostly, I like the security that comes with being a waitress. While scientists, teachers, construction people, and trained technicians are standing in unemployment lines, I am still working. I could go into any strange town and within two weeks be working at least a few hours a week.

"I know I'll always be able to take care of myself. I have come a long way since that scared little housewife and mother who thought she needed a husband to support and protect her. I've married again, and my husband would like to take me away from all this, but I haven't been able to sever the ties that bind me to the job. I have a good marriage, but I never want to be completely dependent on anyone again!"

The Education of Eddi Frederick

As she approaches thirty, Eddi Fredrick is still not sure just what she wants to do with her life. She holds two bachelor's degrees—one in the writing of poetry—and she is credentialed to teach elementary school. For Eddi, waitressing is not a way of life, but rather a way station while she sorts her pieces another time and tries to decide what life course to choose. The pleasure she takes from waitressing comes not from the work itself, but from what she sees and learns about human nature, including her own, every day.
—L.R.

EDDI FREDRICK
(Posh hotel overlooking a seaside city)

"I enjoy the closeness amongst the waitresses. I think it comes from suffering the same indignations and receiving the same pleasures.

"As for the customers, I don't like them as well in the morning as I do in the afternoon. People are very peculiar in the morning and they forget that I just woke up too. They want their coffee, lots of coffee, and they are crabby until they get it. People have the weirdest breakfast habits; they invent weird combinations—powdered sugar and berries or melon and honey.

Everything is such a big decision—*one* egg, *one* piece of toast, *one* piece of bacon. And they have these amazing and very serious rituals about eating their eggs—everything from using catsup on scrambled eggs to dipping their toast in fried-egg yolks. To me an egg is an egg, but because this is a fancy place, they come in all dressed up expecting something exciting. Sometimes they even want breakfast served in courses.

"You have a funny kind of power working in a fancy place. Sometimes, the customers think you must be as classy as the restaurant and they want to impress you with their good manners. After all, what else are manners for?

"I can tell when people know how to order and when they don't. For example, if they are looking at the prices, they probably shouldn't eat in such an expensive place. When people keep ordering more bread, you know it is not so much that they like the bread, but they are trying to fill up because it's free. I know when people order spinach salads because they love spinach salad and I know when they're cheap or afraid to try anything new. Sometimes I say, 'We usually serve that as an appetizer, it is very small.' Also, I won't make much if they order small things, so I try to sell them and applaud them for eating a lot or trying new things, like the manta ray. When I first started, I would get so excited when people ate the best things, I would say, 'Oh, good.'

"I haven't served any Conga fish, but then I don't know much about it. I don't think anyone outside of the Cousteau Society knows much about the Conga fish. The chef brought it out of the freezer and it looks about seven feet long and is a cylindrical creature, much like a big, fat eel. We also serve sturgeon, a very ugly freshwater fish that is endangered, no less.

"Our chef is innovative, you might say; people come a hundred miles to sit on this hill and eat something fancy. It's a total experience.

"Nouvelle portions are small but beautiful to look at, pleasing to taste. One man said, 'Nouvelle, hell. This isn't enough to fill up a midget.' I said that I guessed the portions were kind of controversial, and he said, 'Controversial, huh? You don't get enough

to eat, you don't come back. Simple as that.' I told my boss and he said, 'If they want to eat a lot, they should go to a smorgasbord.'

"Our people always have quiche, always. Once when somebody asked, 'What kind of Quiche Lorraine do you have today?' my tongue slipped and I said, 'We have the Lorraine Lorraine.'

"For uniforms, we wear the modified tuxedo. Polyester, rain or shine, and when the weather is hot, it's a little torture chamber. Before opening every day, we all line up and the maitre d' looks us over, checks our aprons, and makes us turn them over if they have a spot on them.

"I enjoy the whole experience of serving food I am proud of in beautiful surroundings. Also, its a good experience to serve; I think everybody should have to serve sometime in their life. Serving is giving, and, as corny as it sounds, it feels good to give. This is one of the main things I am learning from this job: I have to humble myself each time I go to a table. Also, the

waitresses all give to each other by pitching in to take care of each other's tables when it gets hectic. The chefs give too; they not only give out food, but they'll help you if you have a special request. And the customer gives too, in kindness and in respect as well as in the tip. Finally, we give back what we have taken during the day by tipping busboys, bartender, and everyone who helped us. It is all so reciprocal. Another thing that I have learned is not to judge people by the tip they give you. I no longer think, 'What crumbs, they on left me ten percent.' I've learned to accept what comes.

"The best tippers are usually men between thirty and fifty who wear designer clothes and dine with other men. Women have a hundred reasons for not tipping well: either you are too pretty or threatening, or they do this at home for free, or they are saving their money to buy something after finishing lunch with their friends.

"I want to say one more thing. I mostly feel elegant about what I am doing, working in a beautiful restaurant; it is not something to be scoffed at. Some people I know act as though I should be just a little embarrassed by doing this, and it makes me angry. I'm learning a great deal about people and giving, and I'm saving material for short stories to write. Also I'm mobile and stimulated by talking to different people everyday—everybody eats out. When I was working as a secretary, it was so confining; you sit there and look at paper and a lot of words. You don't move around much and you drink a lot of coffee. With waitressing, there is always something new to see, to learn."

At Ease at the Officers' Club

Here is waitressing at its most orderly and predictable. Everything runs like clockwork, meal times are exact, and the "guests" are of the same persuasion. In this coffee shop with an air of pretense, rank and decorum prevail—there is never any commotion. The waitresses, however, have great rapport and bawdy laughter sometimes bursts through the swinging doors from the kitchen.

—L.E.

COLLEEN SAUNDERS

"A man asked what I did with my tips. I told him I buy things like bread and milk, so he left me twenty-five cents. The money is not great here, but the hours are good for me and for my three kids. It's hard work too; it took me two months to get my legs in shape for this job.

"My husband is an officer and there's some stigma to my working here. People think it's more of an enlisted man's wife's job. I discussed it with my husband and we decided that, since it's honest work, there's nothing wrong with it. Still, a lot of people feel like I've betrayed the system: we're not supposed to be associated with enlisted people. There are a lot of unwritten rules in the military."

CORA SCOTT

"Seating people can be crazy. People have phobias about where to sit—not by a wall, not facing a corner, not in the middle of the room. It's further complicated here because of rank, which puts extra pressure on everybody. Then there's always someone claiming to be a friend of the admiral and wanting the best table in the house.

   "Besides rank, there's another heirarchy with the fighter pilots on top, the helio pilots on the bottom, and the administrative officers, the 'desk pilots,' somewhere in the middle."

Kris laue

"We have family night from time to time and the little kids take over and run wild. I was carrying a heavy tray loaded with six dinners when one of the kids tripped and crashed into me, dumping one of the dinners on a woman in a tweed jacket. What a sight, with french fries stuck in her collar."

Monica insteness

"My husband only signed up for two years. He's an enlisted man so he's not allowed to visit here. Even if he takes his discharge I plan to continue on here. We have good job security, good benefits, which makes up for the fact the tips are poor. As a matter of fact, the higher the rank, the lower the tip."

Bonnie Rembert

"Before this I worked in a huge room at another Navy Base. It seemed like a football field and sometimes I had to wait on close to a hundred people. When I left, they gave me a picture of myself with roller skates on.

"Part of waitressing is getting out of the house. I love my children and my home, but I was going bananas staying in the house all the time. I really don't have to work, but I want to: meeting people keeps me happy. I don't just wait on people, I talk to them. And you can be sure I'm not here because of the food; I took some scraps home to my dog and he just turned up his nose."

Sandy Houghton

"You don't see their military side when you're
serving them, and you don't have to salute.
The wives can be unbearable, however.
They wear their husbands' rank smack in
the middle of their foreheads."

Deborah Williams

"I grew up in South Bend, Indiana, but my boyfriend used to beat me, so I came as far west as possible and have been here now almost six years. I didn't have a car for six months, but my sister waitresses saw to it that I got back and forth to work every day.

"This is the best job I've ever had. I've worked in places where it really wasn't peaches and cream. We're kind of all like family here. Our boss wouldn't let anybody treat us bad. If someone gives us a hard time, he backs us up. His attitude is, 'These are my waitresses, and if you don't like it then just hit the door.' Sometimes he's hard to work for; sometimes he yells and makes us feel little, but you're all going to have days like that.

"I'm in a talent show at the community center where I do creative dance and never do the same moves twice. I really like waiting on tables too. What I like best is

being nice to people and having them be nice back. It's almost like I feel when I dance—all the response."

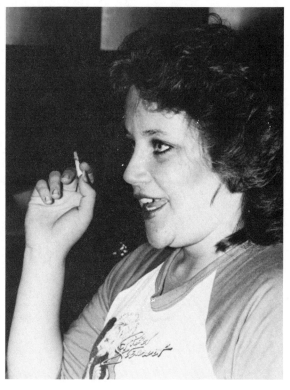

Sandy Beatman

"I have to admit, my parents were right. If I had gone through college I'd be something other than a sandwich girl right now. I'd counsel a young person to go straight through school. All I used to do was party and get high. I really want a good career—to be an engineer or something. Oh, I like waitressing, but I don't want to make a career of it."

JANET McGANN

"When we get paid we say, 'The eagle shit.'"

Breakfast with Tracie

Although not yet twenty-one, Tracie is a five-year veteran on the breakfast shift and has developed a precocious perception of people, particularly early-risers. She's a bundle of energy and enthusiasm, street wise, and has a flair for conversation. The future is hers. All she has to do is name it.

—L.E.

TRACIE VASSALLO
(A respected motel-restaurant)

"I get myself psyched up for my job. The alarm goes off at 4 a.m. and plays rock at full blast. I get right into the shower to wake up and drive to work with the radio on loud. The cook gets here first and I have to pound on the door because he can't hear above the sound of frying bacon. When I get inside the first thing I do is make a pot of coffee and turn up the music. Busboy sets the tables, I make more coffee, cut the cantaloupe, make iced tea, fill the creamers, cut grapefruit, lemons, fill the condiments, and check the wine list. Then the other waitress comes, then the hostess, and at seven comes the third waitress. Last comes the owner.

"First customers are the regulars. Then I have those who come here for the morning and drink anywhere from six to twenty cups of coffee and read the paper. Maybe that's when we should start charging rent. I never ask them to leave, but I will ask if there's anything more and start wiping up around them.

"I'd rather wait on regulars than strangers. They like me. It's a compliment when they ask for my station. They are young and old and male and female—all sorts. We get a lot of businessmen, thirty-five and older, for *breakfast*. They either live alone or else eat out so they won't bother anyone. I know what this one wants—black coffee with Sweet & Low and I have it ready even before he sits down.

"I have two people who come in every Saturday and order pancake sandwiches. When I see them coming I put in their order. One day they called me over and said they'd like to change their order, and there it was, waiting to be served. The cook got mad and ate the pancake sandwich himself; he eats twenty-four hours a day.

"Difficult people come in sometimes, like when there's a horse show in town; fifty percent of them are snobby and they make you seem like you're dirt. This flashy woman came in wearing an expensive western suit and asked for food to go, which means all these bags and foil wrap and plastic plates. Here I am, waiting on the

whole counter alone, and when I hand her the bags she peeks inside and says, 'I don't want those plastic utensils. How can I get regular silverware?' I tell her, No, that for food to go it just isn't done. So she said, 'Well, miss, I don't like this clam chowder, I want the other kind.' Then she went on— get me this , get me that, I don't like this and I don't like that. I exchanged the soup and she planted it on the counter. Remember, each minute of waitressing is valuable, especially when you're busy. Then she said, 'I just don't want anything. Just forget it.' She was mad and I just started to cry. When they get out of hand I feel lost.

"There was another thing I couldn't handle. An older man didn't look so well and was sweating a lot. He slumped in his booth with his eyes closed and I called the paramedics. They came and put him on a stretcher while people around were saying, 'More coffee, please,' or 'Can you take my order now?' I got upset. One of the older waitresses came over and said, 'Now just stop sniffling and take care of your customers. Things like this happen, but you have to dry your tears and get back to work.'

"There's a single woman who comes in from nearby and sometimes has two lunches, like she forgot she was here an hour before. Once she came in with her coat on but nothing underneath. She had just forgotten, and she was living alone. She worked her whole life in a department store and was a spinster to the end.

"Then there was another older woman who just sat there with her soup and peed. It just happened like she didn't know what was happening. Then she paid and left. I think it's kinda sad.

"There was a scary time when a guy in booth forty-two was playing with himself. The other waitresses saw what he was doing too, and nobody wanted to get near him. It took another guy to come along and bounce him out of there for us.

"A lot of older people like to tell me about their trip to Greece or wherever, and show me pictures and tell me family gossip.

"I'm kind of an information center for tourists—they ask me about the weather, where to go, what to do, what to eat. So I tell them what I can. But sometimes something gets into me and I'll send them off in the wrong direction. I don't feel mean, it's more a prank.

"Older women are pickier than older men. The women will complain about the salad dressing and want it on the side, but the men don't care. Maybe it's because a man has been cooked for all his life and has learned not to complain.

"What bugs me is when I got to a table of four traveling businessmen and two order coffee, and I serve it, and the third then decides he wants coffee and I bring it, then a friend joins them and he gets his. Then after the same in food ordering, they suddenly announce they want separate checks.

"When somebody doesn't like the way the chicken is cooked, the trick is not to get caught in the crossfire between customer and cook. What you say in that case is, 'She likes her chicken more well done.' You never say, 'You didn't cook this the way she ordered it.' Offend the cook and all hell breaks loose.

"Even in later years, if I'm married with a

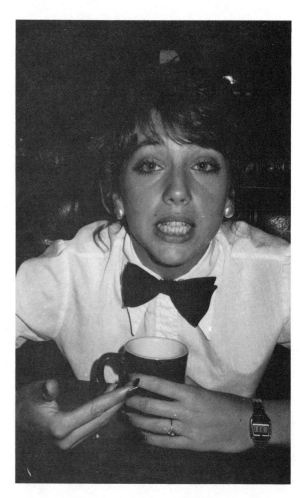

couple of kids and being provided for, I'd still like to be a waitress again. I like the interplay with people. And I don't take things personally as I did in the beginning; my tears have pretty well dried up."

Enduring Friends

Most of the waitresses in this group have become my friends and go for a pair of draft beers when they see me coming. They know I like to let one "breathe." I know some of their idiosyncracies, too. One of them keeps an extra ballpoint jabbed under an ankleband, though she's never had to use it. Another wears a wig. I won't tell who. The point is, in spite of a certain amount of cafe-hopping on both our parts, we see each other regularly over a span of years and I suppose if you added up all the hours, they'd fill up a few weeks of our lives.

—L.E.

DENISE TAYLOR
(Popular bar-restaurant)

"When I see you coming there's never any question in my mind what you want. I'll never forget the day you forgot who you were and ordered a rum and coke."

L INDA GRIM
(Family restaurant)

"At first I was reluctant to appear in this book...for one thing, my husband thinks I work in a bank. Gold mine is closer to the truth."

DEE-DEE ABSTON
(A bustling restaurant, hometown favorite)

"I don't like waiting on tourists from New York or France—they're so demanding. New Yorkers are pushy and expect fantastic food wherever they go. I can take more abuse from men than I can from women. I'd say, on the whole, that gay men are some of the best tippers.

"Nicky the waiter gets bigger tips because he's a man and is seen as the head of a family. It burns me up because so many waitresses are divorced and raising families.

"The new plates here are bigger and heavier than the old ones: I can only carry three instead of five. But I can't expect the owner to throw out ten thousand dollars worth of china because of that —or can I?

"Last night I had a spat with the bartender. He said, 'See that door. If you don't like the way I tend bar, don't let it hit you on the ass on your way out.' I ran off crying."

BARBARA LONG
(Head waitress)

"Ten years ago I was forced to wear red hot pants, a red halter, and cheap red plastic platform boots that gave me hammertoe.

"It was the newest steak house in town and was quite the rage for a while. They prided themselves on their 16-ounce top sirloins, but the plates weighed even more. I had two couples in the corner booth, furthest from the kitchen. Lighting was dim and everything was maroon—the carpet, the upholstery, and even the walls.

"I was experienced with cocktails, but not carrying three heavy plates on one arm and the fourth in the other hand. I was nervous enough without the manager lurking around, eyeing me. As I approached the booth my arm gave out and the three plates went flying. What a commotion. As the busboy rushed over to help he hit the table and knocked over their tall drinks. Everything was everywhere! The customers jumped up and brushed themselves off and disappeared to the restrooms to give us time to clean up.

"Finally, the busboy and I thought we had everything all squared away and I'm standing there smiling as the people came back. The ladies were in satin dresses and scooched in first. The one of them let out a scream and jumped up. She had sat smack down on one of the steaks. Sounds funny now, but it cost me my job."

DEBORAH WRIGHT
(A cosmically conscious vegetarian restaurant)

"My first job involved doing both the cooking and the waiting. I was nineteen at the time and the man who was to be my husband walked in for dinner. He was an old man, about 29. He came in when I was the only one there and he knew, when he saw me, he was going to marry me. He had this romantic picture of this lady behind the counter serving him dinner for the rest of his life. It was all his vision; I had nothing to say about it. After I got married, I had children and gave up waitressing for a long time.

"A lot of people don't recognize me when they see me off duty. When I take off my uniform, I'm a different person, even to those I work with."

ANNIE PEERY
(A family restaurant in the full sense of the word)

"We're just one great big happy family here—
my mom, sister, brother, sister-in-law, me,
and about fifty more who are related by
vocation."

Nancy

The Family
*that steered its restaurant straight into
the hearts of a thousand ardent regulars.*

Luverna

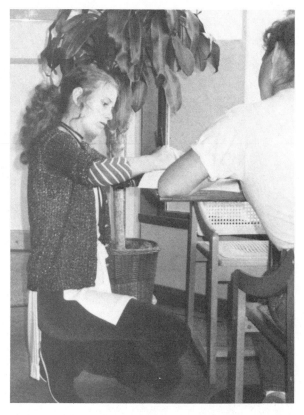

KIMBERLY
(A small lunchroom)

"Kneeling is my style because I don't like to tower over people when I'm taking their order. It doesn't mean I'm humble either, it's my way of getting with it."

PAGE
(A fledgling cafe)

"It amazes me sometimes how many trips it takes to serve someone a simple lunch."

PATRICIA MAMMANO
(Businessman's lunch at noon, watering hole at night)

"At one time or another, everyone who has worked as a waitress has experienced the waitress nightmare. Work dreams are usually the unpleasant result of anxiety felt by responsible employees who want to perform well even under the sometimes impossible demands of the job. Restaurant dreams can reflect the exaggerated frustration, confusion, low self-esteem and sometimes plain hysteria that can be a part of this often stressful and unappreciated work. Even upon awakening, we may be so obsessed with getting that man his long-awaiting drink, we may feel momentarily obligated to go back into the dream. In my years of waitress nightmares, I have found myself working against every imaginable obstacle: an unfamiliar labyrinth of a restaurant, a full station completely unset-up, unintelligible, indecisive and, of course, demanding customers. Celebrities appear who insist on obscure cocktails; friends show up at the busiest moment expecting special attention. I am often ill-prepared, late, undressed, paralyzed, intoxicated or unable to speak. In one dream I forgot my pen and had to use my fingernail to etch inscrutable orders into the palm of my hand. In another, I tried to answer a customer only to discover my mouth filled with old gritty tea leaves. Once, the guilt of a late and then spilled order became so horrendous, the sky darkened, sirens screamed, and a ten-foot-tall policeman appeared to administer my punishment. But my favorite of these mounting frustration dreams culminated with my tossing a half-liter of house white at the manager and flying away up through the ceiling grate, escaping the whole angry scene.

"However, I believe these dreams reflect the purely physical rebellious side of what we imagine to be servitude. Ironically, in the free time allowed me by waitressing, I have come to understand that part of the maturing process is to learn that to serve others selflessly can be a goal in itself. In our materialistic, upward-mobility-oriented society, many who are so caught up in their careers never find the time to discover for themselves the truths that give life meaning. Once understood, dreams, even waitress nightmares, can be a part of the whole healing process."

ROBIN ROWE
(A smart art-deco restaurant)

"I think of waitressing as a way station in my life. I hope to be a career geologist someday, but that means graduate school, which means more waitressing. A means to an end."

LISA LINDQUIST
(A smart new restaurant)

"Some people love to be ill-treated, but I don't have the heart."

BOZANNA "BETSY" POVOL
(A busy and boisterous old-fashioned restaurant)

"My parents were working people who immigrated from Czechoslovakia. I got my first waitress job at a drugstore counter when I was eighteen for forty-three cents an hour. I was a single parent with two children at that tender age; I had to have money every day for survival and waitressing was it.

"Nights here bring a loud, rude crowd. But I got used to all the bad language and I can always swear back in Czech and no one knows. The only fight I ever saw here was between some out-of-town firefighters. I just ran and hid until it was over.

"Sometimes there's an under-ager with older friends and they try to order drinks for him. Well, I just say, 'You know the rules.' I know what they'll do when my back is turned, so I'll have another waitress or the hostess or even the busboy keep an eye on that table. Otherwise, we'd all get busted.

"I can usually tell, just by looking, when people are not from this country. I don't know what it is—the dress, the hair style, something different. Sometimes they don't seem to know a word of English either and I just guess at what they want and it usually works out. Europeans always want their meat well done and french fries or spaghetti instead of baked potatoes. Except for Argentina and maybe Australia, we're the only steak-eating country in the world. When they see the size of the steaks they say, '*That* much?'

"All of us working here are old pals. We all tried having a picnic once, but it got rained out."

D EBBIE LIPSON
(Country western bar and bowling)

"No windows and everybody smoking! I hear that secondhand smoke is worse than the original stuff. I've gotten good at switching ashtrays, but still I go home reeking from the smoke and the greasy buffet, which includes catsup, mustard and chili sauce. Shedding my uniform doesn't help; the smell gets in my skin and hair. It takes a head-to-toe cleansing to leave the bar behind.

"I sometimes wonder if my uniform could be vacuum-packed and sent to starving people somewhere—after a good boiling it should yield up a healthy soup."

MARY ANNE SCHMIDT
(Cocktail lounge with veranda)

"A cocktail waitress needs a photographic memory, but I don't have one, alas. That's why I sometimes seem to be daydreaming. Actually, I'm trying to remember who wanted the grasshopper in a tall glass, who had the Turkey in a Bucket, who wanted onions instead of olives, who had the double twist, and what gentleman asked for the tour map, and about a dozen other drinks as well. My legs may put in ten miles, my arms will lift a hundred trays, but it's my brain that gets exhausted."

DONNA HENDERSON
(A noisy, comfortable restaurant drawing a cross-section crowd)

"I'm an ex-high school art teacher, actually, but I didn't like the regimentation. Waitressing gives me more freedom and flexibility. I take home money every day and have time to paint.

"Something else—I never get bored here. It's a wonderful human zoo. Sometimes I see women picking up tips their husbands left—real sneaky."

R UTH COVELL
(Courtyard cafe)

"Although it goes against my nature, sometimes I have to play the cop and check IDs. So here's this seventeen-year-old girl with three legal people and they're all giving me a bad time for not serving her. They're giving her sips behind my back, yet I'm liable for a $500 fine and a morals charge. They got belligerent and left me an eighteen-cent tip on a $30 tab. Yet you gotta keep on smiling."

MAGGIE JAMES
(A national chain)

"My first job was at the opening of a new Howard Johnson's and we were given hounds-tooth uniforms that made us feel frumpy. The manager said they were designed in Paris, which was a laugh. Even though we had a week's training, none of us was prepared for the mob scene. One girl couldn't take it. She had six full dinner plates on a tray and had to maneuver through a crowd. First one plate skittered to the edge and she just watched it go off and hit the floor. With the tray unbalanced, she overcompensated and lost two more. Another lunge, another plate, and one by one they all hit the floor. She simply threw up her hands and said, 'It's all yours,' and we never saw her again."

POPPET HILL
(A raucous saloon)

"I work on both sides of the bar, depending on whose night off it is. I like it both ways. The work is harder as a waitress, but at least you're free to move around. Behind the bar you can get trapped.

"My first work was in England. Over there they're much more class conscious and a waitress isn't in high regard. Here, you get the illusion of being freer but there are cliques, dearie, hidden cliques."

ANGIE CALIGIURI
(Italian lunch and dinner house)

"I've worked both sides of the fence. I began as an owner for my father, then went off on my own as a waitress for some years, and now I've got this place. Everyone's been here for at least a year, more than a lot of restaurants can say. The turnover can be ferocious, but not here. I never ask anyone to do something I wouldn't do myself. Thing is, there's nothing I haven't done."

JOY AVOLIO
(A small struggling cafe)

"My first waiting was in Spain when I was seventeen. I was a bartender on the Costa del Brava that dealt mostly with tourists from Europe. They came in waves—the French in June, followed by the Germans. In July the English and the Scandinavians came.

"Later I became a hostess on a very exclusive floating barge under the Brooklyn Bridge. I seated Princess Grace and many celebrities. It was common to get a hundred-dollar tip for giving someone a window seat.

"We had the best-fed cats in town. They lived on shrimp and lobster only. Never knew what catfood was."

Waitresses from Afar

Must of us are drawn to the exotic, which helps to explain the enduring popularity of foreign restaurants in our towns and cities. I am no exception and have always been curious about waitresses from other countries who have come here and taken jobs to serve Americans on their own turf. Some of them blend right into our steak-house culture, while others retain their exotic mien and work in ethnic restaurants. Many that I encountered had experience in both cultures and I was interested in any comparisons they cared to volunteer. Serving people, I learned, is not the same the world over. We can eat in a dozen tongues while speaking only one. —L.E.

ANAT SHARABY
(Small cafe serving "enlightened food of the Middle East")

"In the Middle East the guest is seated at the head of the table and we keep filling his plate until food is left. I want everyone here to feel he's the king and fill him up too.

"People coming here are eager for new things. It's exotic, an adventure in eating. My Yemen spice, for example, has fourteen different ingredients. But in Israel this would just be typical and people would be more critical. Ah, there's so much more freedom here."

NORMA LOPEZ
(Mexican family restaurant)

"Lopez is my married name, but I'm really black Irish. I've been a waitress ever since I was a kid. I've been in all kinds of places, but this is the best. There's a family atmosphere here. I'm not just a waitress, I'm representing 'the family.'

"The kitchen help is all from Mexico so I had to learn to write my orders in Spanish. When I start complaining, the cooks give me hot plates without warning. I get about four steps away and then it hits me. I yell, 'Holy Chihuahua!'

"I like to lay out food on the plate so it looks good; so an onion looks like an onion, the tomato is red, chile is green, so when I set it down directly in front of the customer I can tell by his face that I'd better come back soon or else the plate will be gone too.

"Queta's a great woman to work for. She's a big-hearted lady with a good word for everyone. She leaves me alone, but does what she can to make my work easier. If there's something wrong, she'll tell me gently.

"Some men were born to be served. They're gentler and give you a little space. Those men you can respond to; they get better service. The machos are hard to deal with."

M YUNG
(Chinese restaurant)

"It's different being a waitress in Korea where
I began. There you don't get tips."

C ORI HOUSTON
(Traditional Japanese restaurant)

"Waitressing has gotten me through college. Putting on a Japanese kimono is play acting. I really get with it sometimes, being 'Japanese' and humble. But all that kneeling got painful so I wear my volleyball kneepads under my costume when serving in the tatami room.

"My most terrifying moment was cooking sukiyaki for a party of four with the oil sputtering in the iron pan and not being adept with chopsticks and afraid I'd be flinging hot onions at the customers.

"The most obnoxious are usually well-dressed middle-aged men who use waitresses as a transference of guilt. He's had a bad time and tells his girlfriend, 'I've had a bad time and now I'll give the waitress a bad time.'"

S HELLY CHIEN
(Chinese restaurant; arrived in the States ten days ago, speaks no English, and is interviewed through CHIN-CHIN CHANG, the owner)

"My husband came first and is the chef here. Now I'm here with him. A chef's wife never goes hungry. We come from Taipei, where most restaurants are four stories high because of the dense population.

"No, I don't like hamburgers and prime ribs so much, so that's why I don't get hungry an hour after an American meal— ha, ha."

S HERRI BETZ
(Small cafe serving "enlightened food of the Middle East")

"My ambition is to be the first haute cuisine female chef on the coast. They laughed in my face when I applied at the Culinary Academy, but I was determined and they let me in."

ROSE SRILEX
(Thai restaurant)

"Traditionally, the meal is served in one trip, even with all the many dishes. But the Americans make me walk more—first the soup, later the salad, like they have all day. And they're always asking how hot is this and that. They have to, I suppose, because the regular American cannot tolerate the hotness.

"You are so generous here. Although there is some tipping in Bangkok, it doesn't happen in the country places.

"Americans always want separate checks. See how we have to work for our tips.

"Watch me fold the napkin—it's called 'bamboo.' It's also a good way to make friends, teaching the bamboo.

"Our old-fashioned Thai style is to eat from cushions on the floor like the Japanese, but in one big room, not closed off. My mother was Burmese. I'm a happy girl.

"Even with pressure in the head, I live it out and keep smiling."

MIEKO (Mickey) DOERKSEN and KYOKO ZITRON

(An exotic Japanese restaurant with sushi bar and tatami room)

"Kyoko and I come from Tokyo and both our husbands are from across the world. Mine was born here but has German blood. The husband of Kyoko came from Sweden. We all like it here. America is more easy going. The customers in Tokyo are more hostile, too many people crowded together.

   "I know people want to eat here and pretend they are in a Japanese temple. We try to make that illusion, but at home I wear jeans and T shirts and I'm a painter, too."

Mme. MATHIEU ODILE
(A friendly French restaurant in California)

"My success comes from inexperience. My mother was the best cook in Alsace-Lorraine, but I think I am better. I choose my waitresses for their inexperience, as long as they have some charm to give to the people."

Yasmeen RAZA
(Pakistani restaurant)

"Waitresses aren't generally accepted in Pakistan. Women aren't supposed to be working, except in teaching, nursing and seamstressing...no tipping over there either—that would be degrading.

"Pakistanis usually sit on the floor on a white sheet and eat from bowls with their right hand. And, of course, no alcohol or juices except for *lassi,* a yoghurt drink.

"I can't confess to being a waitress here. I'm just helping my brother, you know, who happens to be the owner.

"If you want service, just snap your fingers."

AILAN "ELLEN" KAO
(Northern Chinese food, Szechuan and Mandarin)

"In the States waitress and customer can be friends, but in China you are a servant— another class. It's a lifetime commitment, particularly for the kitchen people.

"Here the waitress gets to show more of her personality, but if something goes wrong she gets the blame. In China, the customer complains to the manager on his way out. It's the customer who usually feels apologetic and even embarrassed.

"In China the waitress stands back and watches her tables from a distance. She won't bother her patrons unless asked.

"It's easier here because Americans don't expect as much. I usually wear long pants because when customers run away without paying, I can chase them.

"My father had a big restaurant in Taiwan, so what else could I do? I really enjoy teaching Americans what real Chinese food is. But certain fresh vegetables don't grow over here, and others the flavor is different because of the soil and climate. It'll never be quite the same."

"Waitresses and other restaurant workers in Taiwan are all full time, especially in the kitchen. They begin to learn their skills very early and have a job for life.

"It is more serious there. People eat out more. There's a kind of philosophy: food comes first! In China a waitress is like a servant. Here a waitress and her customer can be friends. Thousands of years of culture makes a difference between you and the people you serve. Here I can joke with anybody.

"Chinese people don't place blame so quickly as here. If something is wrong they take more responsibility and don't make a fuss. It is even an embarrassment for them as well as the waitress.

"Americans are pickier, but the Chinese demand more respect."

ANGIE SEVILLA SOLIS
(Mexican bar in a farming town)

"This is a small town. They call it a second Peyton Place. Sometimes my customers know about me before I know about me. I like working with men. They make me feel good. They notice things, your hair, the colors you're wearing. I like it. I'm a Leo and Leos like attention.

"Sometimes new faces feel like they have to make a pass. I just set them straight and we become good friends.

"I was eighteen when I started working. I started in the dime store, then went to a Taco Bell. I took some years off and had six kids. Now that I've learned bartending, there's nothing else I'd rather do. They call us bartenders The Listeners. We hear their problems, their advice and tell them jokes. This is even my hangout on my days off."

S AN YEU CHAN
(Dim Sum restaurant in a Chinatown)

"I think I'm getting rich fast, but I know it's only an illusion. I like the illusions of America." *(Translated by the head waiter.)*

Reluctant Confessions

L IN ROLENS

"I never wanted to be a waitress, but there I was, a nineteen-year-old university dropout and I had never worked a day in my life. Not a day. Doing my own laundry and ironing the fronts of my shirts in my freshman year was about it. I had not made my bed, done dishes, vacuumed, or, God forbid, cleaned a bathroom in my entire indulged life. Though my family was solidly middle class, it had been made clear to me early that there were two kinds of people in this world: those who served and those who were served. My function was to be served.

"At nineteen, I was unemployed and virtually unemployable. My top typing speed was twenty-seven words a minute on a good day; I thought dictation was what happened under despots, and filing was what you did to your nails. That left, according to the local job calendar, two options: motel maid and waitress. The choice was not difficult.

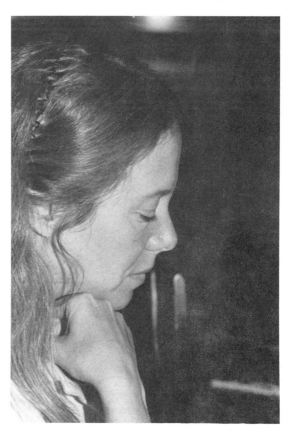

Each involved serving and the pay was lousy, but waitresses worked around food and people rather than domestic refuse, and tips were rumored to be the pot of gold at the end of the daily rainbow.

"I landed my first waitress job using the techique revered by all first-time waitresses: I lied. I fabricated a story about having worked in an Oregon coffeeshop one summer while staying with my grand-parents. Though they hired me, their illusions of my competence must have faded the first time I appeared in the aqua (it was a seafood restaurant) polyester uniform with the Peter Pan collar.

"I was lucky that day. The manager had just started a long weekend and the cook was in charge. For an hour, I stumbled around in fashionable flats trying to remember who had shrimp cocktail and who had oysters on the half shell and what kind of fork to serve with each, trying to make sure that my single table had enough coffee and cream and sugar and iced tea and lemon and tartar sauce and shrimp sauce and catsup and sour cream, and then cleaning up after the two-year-old who had dumped his milk into the platter of halibut sitting in front of the lady to his right.

"I was on the verge of tears. The cook took me aside and suggested that maybe this was enough for my first day. Why didn't I take the rest of the afternoon off and buy myself some sensible shoes, and then come in an hour early tomorrow so he could show me a few short cuts.

"That man saved my life. When I presented myself the next morning, blistered feet wrapped in orthopedic-looking nurse's shoes, he took me under his wing. He demonstrated how to save time and steps and how to carry things efficiently. He made very sure I knew how to maintain control of a party of diners, rather than the other way around. He told me stories of veteran waitresses who had delivered steaming lobsters into the laps of ladies in evening gowns. And he solemnly explained the importance of getting along with cooks, who, after all, could make you or break you in this business.

"By the time the manager had finished his weekend, I could make my way around the dining room without embarrassing anybody, and I had even started to like what was to become my bread and butter for the next ten years.

"To say that I have had a variety of experience is perhaps an understatement. After my seafood job, I worked as the pea-and-carrot girl in a large dormitory, standing next to my boyfriend, the fries-or-mashed man.

"I worked for several years at the Santa Barbara airport coffeeshop, where there were two people and four jobs and we bargained daily over the division of labor among cook, waitress, bartender, and dishwasher. Usually this worked well until the fog rolled in and suddenly sixty frustrated people clamored for gin and cheeseburgers. My first job in such cases was to stand on a chair and announce that we were all in this together and it would all work out if only they could be patient and cooperate.

"I worked at Willy's Rock and Soul on the Berkeley/Oakland border and served chitlings, black-eyed peas, and bar-b-que to local blacks and wayward liberals.

"I made a brief appearance at The Fire House, where the hostess checked our table settings with a ruler and we were required to slide down the firepole in the center carrying a miniature cake and singing happy birthday.

"I hustled beers at the Orchid Bowl to thirsty, good-natured bowlers, and I served watered cocktails in a smokey over-forty bar where the three-piece band wore wine polyester suits with ruffled shirts.

"At Jacque's European Style Family Restaurant, I wore red, white, and blue striped hot pants and served seven continental courses to local gourmands. Amid the early whorehouse splendor of flocked red-velvet wallpaper and red-vinyl booths, my primary concern was to keep several steps ahead of the gay head waitress known to all as Hands.

"I spent nine pleasant months working in a family-owned Italian restaurant in Berkeley and cheerfully gained fifteen pounds on homemade Italian sausage and cheese sandwiches. I learned to deal with the local crazies, including the flasher (democratically, at each table) and my favorite, who always ordered two dinners and carried on fascinating conversations with his invisible friend.

"In a moment of desperation, I served canned soup and soggy grilled cheese sandwiches at a dimestore counter while wearing one of those horrible translucent seersucker uniforms. I discovered that people ate on those rickety stools not because it was cheaper, but because it was insulting. My job was not to serve but to insult, to demean where possible. People tipped better for it and the management took sudden interest in my potential.

"I opened an omelette house, where my responsibility was to make five gallons of fresh fruit salad between 5:30 and 6:00 each morning. I spent the rest of the day pouring coffee and sticking to myself.

"Near my university, I carried beer and pizza at a side-street place managed by a fading Dodger hero. The departments came in groups: chemistry drank the most, the philosophy and English departments tended to play with their food, and the physicists laughed to themselves as though they knew secrets and were not about to tell.

"It has been seven years since I last waited tables and I still miss it. Though I worked my way through six years of university, most of my useful education I received while waiting tables. To this day, I can spot a turkey sandwich when it walks through the door."

The Eight Percent "Solution"

The waitress world was thrown into a turmoil in 1983 when the federal government, clamping down on unreported tips, levied an eight-percent tax on reported tips. The money was deducted from paychecks by the employers who were obliged to declare eight percent of their gross sales as tips unless, through an appeal to the IRS, they could demonstrate a below-average tip rate.

Los Angeles Times

Jess Unruh, the California State Treasurer, once said, "Money is the mother's milk of politics." In the heat of protest against the new tax, a waitress told me that that tip was her "mother's milk." Working for minimum wage, she found her meager paycheck further eroded. Demonstrations flared up all over the country; petitions for repeal choked the mailboxes; the new law's unfairness was decried. Critics showed this was another tax-rate structure that forced people in the lowest economic bracket to pay federal taxes when their income was as low as $60 a week—clearly below poverty level. A spokesman for the Culinary Alliance declared that eight percent was much too high for restaurants catering to pensioners and in poverty-level neighborhoods where tipping averaged less than five percent.

The Los Angeles Times *printed the testimony of Linda McLaughlin, a thirty-five-year-old single mother of a boy, twelve, who claimed the new law put a stranglehold on her bill-juggling system, something she was able to manage before the new law. When she had to choose between paying the rent for her apartment and the phone bill, her phone was disconnected.*

Another waitress, Linda Armstrong, said she took home about $20 in tips for each six-hour day, but that her paycheck, for three days a week, has gone from $38 a week to $23, and that child care alone costs about $12 a day for her two youngsters. "My pay covers the groceries only. If I stopped working, though, I couldn't afford the necessities, even if I took care of my own kids. I need every dollar I earn."

In the face of the furor, the government wouldn't budge. The IRS called this one of the most poorly understood and controversial tax requirements in history. Yet it stressed that not much is new. Waitresses have always been required to report tip income to their employers, who have always been required to withhold taxes on the income. Now, in addition to this process, restaurants must compare reported tips against total sales. If the total tip income reported by all the employees is less than eight percent of total sales, the restaurant must allocate the difference among the employees. This allocation shows up on the W-2 form. Small cafes can ignore all this. The requirement only affects restaurants with a payroll of more than eighty employee hours per day.

Two years after passage of the law, it became accepted as another rigor in the career of a waitress.   —L.E.

Other Voices—Busy Hands

LOUISE BAILEY
(Twenty-four hour motel coffeeshop)

"I came out here from Nashville, then my husband and I split up and I had to support my boys. I went to truck driving school so I could travel with my boyfriend, but then we broke up.

"I like waiting on men. I've always liked men; that was one of the great things about truck driving school.

"We get a lot of transient people off the street, people on drugs and the like. Sometimes we have to ask them to leave. Still, I like the people here better than any I've ever met—regular people off the street. After all the lawyers and movie stars I've waited on, these common people are a pleasure for me. They're friendly and real, and that's what life's all about."

AMY FERGUSON
(Bar-restaurant for the younger crowd)

"I prefer dinner houses where you control the table. You have a captive audience for the evening. Let's face it, a waitress is an entertainer.

"I've worked banquets, but it's too impersonal. But you can't knock the money—not when you're getting a dollar a head for fifty people plus cocktail tips."

"I swear that waiters and waitesses are the toughest people to wait on; they know what they want and what they can get and they can be really demanding. For them, medium rare means medium rare, and a dry martini should be just that. And they want all the condiments, everything. But let me tell you, they tip.

"One day I had a party of four older waitresses, real old pros. The airport coffeeshop was the first stop on the Hawaiian vacation they were taking together. They all drank a couple of drinks, I think it was martinis and stingers, and they then had cheeseburgers—cheeseburgers! I ran for those women for an hour and a quarter: more of this and clean napkins and did we have any French mustard. They drove me crazy. But they had a good time and when they left, there was a five or ten dollar bill tucked under each plate. They made my day."

REBECCA OSWALD
(Majestic Spanish restaurant with an inner courtyard, balconies and mariachis)

"What I remember most about working there was when the tour buses would pull up and unloose all these little old ladies who never heard of enchiladas, and they all brought their own tea bags wanting hot water, please, and no tips."

"One place I worked, we had a good-natured, tough old waitress who took dozens of vitamins with each meal and smoked Gauloise. She didn't take anything off anybody and when some jerk just wouldn't treat her like a human being, she'd smile her warmest smile, look directly into the guy's eyes and say, 'Fuck you very much, sir.' They could never quite believe they'd heard it."

"I remember being so infatuated with one of my customers who came in (I longed and hoped) to see me, that my hands would shake as I took him his coffee. I would have to hold the cup carefully in one hand and the saucer in another in an attempt not to fill the saucer with steaming coffee."

"No one talks about it much, but it's pretty well known around town that cops eat for free or at least for cheap. Every place I've ever worked, there's been some kind of "professional discount" for the local police. In one town, the local chief was a German, full-sized when I met him, who loved to eat. And the woman who ran the place did well by him. She fed him double cheeseburgers slathered in homemade chili. And, when he had started to blossom, she served him huge chef salads with turkey, ham, roast beef, and two kinds of cheese all topped by a full cup of big-chunked bleu cheese dressing. That man bought a new set of uniforms every year. Everytime he left, he left a little fatter and a little happier."

The Last Laugh

MAMIE ROBLES
(Old Italian dinner restaurant)

"I'll never know what it's like to work anywhere else. Oh my, I began here twenty-six years ago and the first thing I learned was to leave my troubles at home. Everyone has troubles. I've had my share, naturally, with raising five kids. When they were young I was working five days a week. Now that they're grown and gone, I've cut back to three. It's cheerful here, food and laughter go together. Jimmy, my boss, and I can always have a good laugh, even after a long hard shift."

Photographer's Credits

Authors Lin Rolens and Leon Elder
reenact their meeting fifteen years earlier.